Weathering Storms

Alice grew up on a farm along the Cork-Kerry border, experiencing a way of life that, though physically demanding, was kind to the land. Now with an awakening sense of environmental issues, we are beginning to look back with a new sense of appreciation on that way of life. In her writing, Alice has endeavoured to create an awareness of the hidden values of the world that respected nature, the divine and people. Her books such as *The Women* and *The Nana* highlight the huge contribution made by women to Irish life. And now in *Weathering Storms,* she writes about the challenges of living well with aging.

For a complete list of Alice's books visit obrien.ie

Weathering Storms

Alice Taylor

Photographs by Emma Byrne

BRANDON

First published 2025 by Brandon, an imprint of The O'Brien Press Ltd.
12 Terenure Road East, Rathgar, Dublin 6, D06 HD27, Ireland.
Tel: +353 1 4923333; Email: books@obrien.ie; Website: obrien.ie
The O'Brien Press is a member of Publishing Ireland.

ISBN 978-1-78849-622-3

The poem on page 35 is from *Familiar Strangers: New & Selected Poems
1960–2004* (Bloodaxe Books, 2004), Brendan Kennelly. Reproduced with
permission of Bloodaxe Books. bloodaxebooks.com

8 7 6 5 4 3 2 1
29 28 27 26 25

Printed and bound by Hussar Books.
The paper used in this book is produced using pulp from managed forests

To the best of our knowledge, this book complies in full with the
requirements of the General Product Safety Regulation (GPSR). For
further information and help with any safety queries, please contact us at
productsafety@obrien.ie.

Cover picture

Uncle Jacky's apple tree, the focal point and special go-to

place in Alice's garden, which grew there for

over a hundred years.

Photo: Emma Byrne

To Gear

who enriches my life with his kindness

Contents

1

Goodbye, Old Friend

Clung to the ground with shock, I simply could not believe my eyes. The whole garden was buried in an avalanche of huge grey branches. They towered above my head. There was no entry point to the garden as all the paths had disappeared under these enormous branches. Covered in grey lichen and ivy, they rose above and beyond my vision. Where on earth had they all come from? And yet, there was something strangely familiar about them, but they belonged in another place, arching high into the sky. Then an ice-cold spark of reality penetrated my shocked stupor, but I went into instant denial. It simply could not be. This just could not have happened. A chilly spark of reality determinedly pierced my numbed brain. There could only be one explanation. These had to be the branches of Uncle

Jacky's apple tree. But what were they doing drowning the entire garden in a tidal wave? What had happened?

I had to find out. I did not want to find out. But I had to. So, with a sense of dread, I forced my way along beside the hedge at the bottom end of the garden, which was the only route through this fallen forest, until I reached the far side. From there I was able to push my way across to where Uncle Jacky's old apple tree had stood for over a hundred years. But not anymore. Her great trunk lay prostrate on the ground and the gaping crater beneath told its own story.

Planted by Uncle Jacky at the beginning of the last century, her branches had been intertwined through his and our lives. She had been the location for Christening, Holy Communion and wedding photographs not only of our family but many village families as well, and in her shade many babies, who had later climbed her, had been sheltered from the sun. In times of pain and struggle she oozed comfort into stressed bodies. She was the go-to place when you came in the garden gate as all paths led to her. On very warm days when it was too hot to sit out in the sun, she provided cooling shade. The table beneath her was the location for solo teas, family gatherings and entertaining visitors. Here the Japanese translator of *To School through the Fields* had marvelled that in her shade he was enjoying an apple cake made from her previous season's apples.

As I stood there remembering, I realised that tears were streaming down my face. Can you grieve for a tree? Now I know that you can. The previous night a storm had rampaged across the country causing devastation, but I thought that my sheltered garden was safe. Now I knew that no place was safe. The heart of the garden, and my old friend and comforter, was gone.

And then I remembered my dream. The night before the storm came I had a strange dream which I am a bit reluctant to write about as some may think that I am crazy, but some things in life are beyond understanding. In the dream I was back in Uncle Jacky and Aunty Peg's old house, now long gone, and opened the door into their little sitting room. Aunty Peg was standing there all dressed in black, which was unusual as she seldom wore black. I felt a spurt of delight on seeing her and ran forward to give her a hug, but she was gone before I reached her. The following morning when I woke up, the dream was still vivid in my mind and I recalled my mother telling me that if you dream of the dead they could be coming to tell you that something is about to happen. Had Aunty Peg come to forewarn me about the tree?

This tree had been interwoven through her life and had provided large crops of apples with which she made pots of apple jelly, jam and her big juicy 'Aunty Peg apple cakes' which I still make every year for the Hospice and Alzheimer's fund-raising days that we hold in my house. She and Uncle Jacky constantly sat beneath it to take a rest during hours of gardening and visitors were taken there to relax after a garden tour. The day Uncle Jacky died Peg sat under it for hours, and many of her friends joined her to chat about him and recall his graciousness and kindness. When they were both gone and the garden came into my care, the seat under Jacky's apple tree became my go-to place where I felt close to them and grateful for the blessings that they had handed on. When life was challenging I sat beneath her and she calmed my turmoil. Other trees and shrubs grew around her but Jacky's apple tree was the queen of the garden.

Every spring she filled the sky with her beautiful apple blossoms and even last summer had produced a large crop of apples. Her early windfalls fed the birds and bees, and the unreachable apples on her top branches continued to feed them for months. A multiplicity of insects and bugs lived along her ivy- and lichen-clad branches and birds nested in her grooves and hollows. A little black skillet pot, hanging off a back branch, provided a family of blackbirds with their water supply. She was truly an Earth Mother. I ran my hand lovingly along her gnarled old trunk in appreciation of all the blessings that she had given us.

Then I needed to share the trauma with someone who would understand, and Eileen, who always seems to be in the right place at the right time, just then came out the back door into the yard. Without telling her what had happened, I led her up into the garden She stood at the gate and gasped in dismay; unlike me, she got it immediately.

'Oh my God, is it Jacky's apple tree?' she asked in a shocked voice. I nodded and led her through my recently created burrow along by the hedge and circled to the far side of the garden until we arrived at the base of the apple tree. It was a sobering sight. 'I can't imagine the garden without it,' I told her. 'It will be very different,' she agreed, and then suggested, 'Wouldn't it be nice if Paddy carved something out of the wood and then you would have some of Jacky's tree forever?' This was such a comforting thought as over the years her husband Paddy, a farmer and wood turner, had created some beautiful things out of wood.

Then Mike, who as a child had gardened here with Jacky, arrived. 'Wow!' he declared, peering into the root pit, 'her roots were pure rotten. Her time was up. That storm had no bother toppling her.' If only I could be as pragmatic as Mike.

Wedged beneath her fallen trunk was one end of the old iron garden seat, which, over the years, had seated so many. It was difficult to know how damaged it was – we would only know that when it was eventually freed. The iron rose bow, or arch, beside her had taken a fair wallop too and was bent over. Would that straighten up? Around her were many battered shrubs and smaller trees. It was a depressing sight so we withdrew to the warm kitchen where Eileen and I had tea.

Later I rang a neighbour with a chainsaw and the gear to clear things up, and enquired about moving the body. That night I rang my sister Phil, a far more knowledgeable gardener that I am, to report and talk over what had happened. After a long discussion she decided, 'Well, if it had to happen, this is the best time of year because in winter you won't be out in the garden as much as you would at other times of the year. And, as well as that, it will give you time to work out the best plan for the way ahead.' I felt better after that phone call as my sister had focused me forwards, which was what I needed just then.

Then early the following morning Paddy came to decide what lengths of timber he would need for his wood turning. 'No problem finding suitable pieces,' he said, 'but it will need a good drying-out period.' 'It will be easier when all this is gone,' I told him, looking at the mountain of fallen branches. 'Yes,' he agreed. And being a farmer added, 'Same as having a dead cow on the farm – the faster it gets moved the better.' True for Macbeth as he contemplated killing the king, Duncan, I thought: 'If it were done when 'tis done, then 'twere well it were done quickly' – though in our case the 'king' was already dead!

So, I was relieved when my friend and his helpers came, and the chainsaw began to whine, and the smaller branches began to be taken out through the gate. With the first bark of the chainsaw the giant trunk rolled off the back of the garden seat, which emerged completely intact. I was so grateful for that. Then when another giant piece of trunk fell off the rose arch, that too tilted back to its former position with the climbing rose still hanging in there. Hopefully in the weeks ahead she, like me, would recover from this upheaval. And the little skillet pot had also survived the crash-landing, so the blackbirds still had their drinking fountain, though in a different location. This old tree, that had grown old gracefully, had now departed in a similar fashion, inflicting as little surrounding damage as possible. In death as in life, she was gracious.

But just as I began to think that the job might get done before evening, the rain came, heavy and persistent, so work had to be abandoned. The following day was Sunday, with a very bad forecast, so all was on hold until Monday. But sometimes life works itself out in ways better than we plan because in retrospect I now know I needed that breathing space before parting with my old friend. We needed time to say goodbye. Not comparing like with like, but maybe that was the wisdom of the old house wakes that could last for days, as this gave people time to absorb the parting. Goodbye takes a long, long time.

2

After the Storm

The lads with the chainsaws had gone and I stood in the garden surrounded by the remains of Jacky's apple tree. Due to bad weather there had been a few days' intermission before they could come back and take down the tree trunk and cut it into more manageable pieces. During those chilly days I walked around the fallen tree hoping that a plan might formulate in my addled brain. Vague ideas assembled and disassembled. But uppermost in my mind was the wish that this old friend in some way or another could sleep peacefully in the garden that she had graced for so many years. But how best to do this? My instinct told me that this was possible, but my brain needed to work out a plan.

Now that the lighter branches were cut up and gone, the beautiful old curving tree trunks were visible and I felt that

by walking around them a solution might emerge. Over the years old tree trunks develop fascinating gnarled and twisted shapes, works of art fashioned by nature. I was surrounded by such pieces. They made for very interesting viewing – some incorporating magnificent, curved elbows and interesting humps and hollows. Their wood-ends were almost like a sunset in colour, with a soft orangey mellow glow. These pieces belonged and deserved to stay in this garden. When I voiced this idea to a pragmatic son, he gave me a questioning look and asked, 'Have you decided that they will see you out?' Maybe I had!

Jacky's apple tree and I had long consultations and eventually a plan emerged. Then came a dry afternoon and the helpers returned, and by then I had a vague plan of action for how to incorporate the tree pieces back into the garden. The helpers had the muscle and strength for the job and I was supposed to have the plan, but it was still a work in progress in my brain. I directed the lads to cut the huge trunks into manageable lengths and though they had no idea what I had in mind, they did everything they could to accommodate what they probably thought was a rather weird process. Their work on fallen trees would normally finish up in a pile of logs for the fire, but not on this occasion. Jacky's apple tree was not for cremation. It would hopefully rest back into the bosom of mother earth here in its home place. That was the plan.

I was very aware that this was no time for dithering or changing your mind in mid-motion as these pieces were heavy ladies. However, some things have the happy knack of working themselves out as they unfold. And that is exactly what happened. We rolled – or rather the two lads rolled – the biggest and heaviest pieces along the paths and many of them found their homes almost by themselves, some as little tables at seat-ends, while others became interesting stand-alone statements at garden corners, and the remainder created unique boundaries around the garden beds. We worked it out as we went along, and gradually I found my rhythm and the two lads got the hang of what I had in mind. As all the pieces slowly found their resting places the huge pile in mid-garden gradually decreased and eventually was no more. Jacky's apple tree was resting all around the garden where she belonged. I was so happy with that.

But the garden still had a battered look. Some of the shrubs were lopsided and needed to be straightened up or pruned back into shape; birds' watering troughs and various garden statuary lay prone all around the place; the paving slabs on which the seat under the tree had rested were upended, and the beds and paths were smothered in debris.

It was time for my buddy and 'tidy-upper', John, to come to my rescue. He arrived next morning bright and early and whizzed into action. He dug up and relaid the paving stones around the tree, and did a super job as usual. He has the innate ability to see what needs to be done and knows how to do it. Back in the home farm whenever my mother needed a thorough yard tidy-up she would term the farm worker who did it to her satisfaction as 'a great shorer'. I

didn't know what that meant but I got the idea – and later discovered the term was used about those workers who built the retaining walls to support the sides of excavations! An important job indeed. My mother's terminology always comes to mind when I see John in action. But I always keep in mind as well that John is no Monty Don and needs to be kept far away from a pruner as he would cheerfully cut the head off you and tell you that you looked much better without it! But as well as being a willing worker he is so funny and witty that working with him is highly entertaining. The ideal man in the present circumstances.

One of my treasured Jacqueline Postill shrubs was filling the garden with her beautiful winter scent though she had been in the line of the tree-fall and had taken a fair battering. Together we pruned it back, with John highly amused that I was actually – at last! – trusting him with a pruner. The Bridal Wreath shrub was totally askew and had to be cut back drastically; it would be interesting to see how well she would recover. Other damaged plants needed a short back-and-sides. With extra light now pouring into the garden a rethink of layout was warranted. This resulted in a lot of shifting and shunting, with some discussion, agreements and disagreements, until finally we were both satisfied with the outcome. John raked up all the debris from the storm and wheelbarrowed it into the trailer that the leader of the chainsaw team had obligingly dropped in that morning. When a calamity happens, good neighbours are a great blessing. Then John cracked into action with his blower, resulting in cleared paths and bringing a sense of order to chaos. Later that evening I breathed a sigh of relief as I walked around the garden, so grateful that Uncle Jacky's apple tree was still there and that the garden was again able to breathe easy. And so was I.

3

Begin Again

With Jacky's apple tree gone, the garden was flooded with light and a huge span of sky became visible. That was the plus side, but the minus side was that the garden now lacked a centrepiece. For so many years the apple tree had been the focus and go-to place when you went in the gate. Now when I went in the gate I was not sure where to look or to turn. So what was best to be done? I was well aware that it would take a lot of thinking and garden research to get this right.

And I was well aware also that as well as making the right choice, time was of the essence because, as one of my sons constantly reminds me when I push my ability boat out too far, 'Mother, remember now, you're no spring chicken.' I needed something that looked good and I needed it now. An old gardener in a hurry? This is a total contradiction in the gardening world. Because there is one ideology that you learn in gardening and that is 'things take time,' a slogan a former headmaster in one of my sons' schools had on his office wall. Which I never forgot. But if that slogan applies in education, it surely applies even more so in gardening. Luckily I had a few winter months to work it out, but I am a 'now' person and needed to get going immediately.

And this old gardener in a hurry did not have time on her side, so I was not prepared to wait. On the other hand, the prospect of the search filled me with excited anticipation. Is there anything a gardener likes better than a space waiting to be filled? But with what? It had to be something of substance, feasible and heart-warming. A tree? But maybe not? Then the crazy thought of moving St Joseph from his perch on the raised bank in front of the Old Hall that shelters the northern side of the garden temporarily came to mind. He has been a welcoming presence there for many years, and now lichen- and moss-covered, he blends beautifully into this old garden. But then common sense prevailed as I remembered the huge challenge it had been to get him into position. Made of Portland stone, he is an enormous weight and when he arrived here many years ago it was possible to trolley him into position, but now, with subsequently added steps and planting, that was not an option. So, St Joseph probably breathed a huge sigh of relief that he had escaped a big shift. Next to come in for consideration was The Foxy Lady, who for years has stood with her back to the high stone wall by the hill. But she was quickly ruled out when

I remembered that on a previous attempted move she had dug her toes into the ground in protest. So that lady was not for moving. A third consideration was a semi-naked lady on a pedestal sheltering in a far corner, but even though the years had softened her with a cloak of moss, this saucy lady was best left in a sheltered corner.

Then I got the most far-fetched idea of all. Last summer at Mallow Garden Show I had seen the most beautiful hare as part of a garden design. I am a big fan of hares. Probably sculpted in bronze, he was breath-taking. Then I tried to visualise him in situ and failed. So, after exhausting a long list of possibilities the conclusion was reached that it takes a tree to replace a tree.

The centre of the garden needed life and Uncle Jacky's apple tree could only be replaced by the right tree. But what was that going to be? My first thought was for a golden frisia, she with the fancy name Robina Pseudoacacia Frisia, one of which I already have in the garden and dearly love as she is like a ray of sunshine. But her branches are so fragile that she now has a Twiggy look – all legs and no body – because her branches crack so easily. Also because she is a bit of a *prima donna* she does not arrive early onto the summer stage.

Then, in order to make a more enlightened choice, I decided to consult my garden encyclopaedias, which proved much more challenging than anticipated. Many years ago when weight-lifting was not an issue, I invested in copies of the *Royal Horticultural Society's Encyclopedia of Gardening*,

which came in three weighty tomes. Back then, lifting these heavy ladies was no problem, but the years have reduced my weight-lifting capacity – and, to make matters worse, a few years ago I used them to raise up a heavy iron lamp to enable it to cast its light around the *seomra ciúin*, my quiet room where I read and think, so there was a bit of serious furniture removal involved too. Accessibility to these knowledgeable ladies now posed a problem which an able-bodied, strong son had to solve. Such are the joys of later years!

After much scanning of pages in one of these weighty ladies my next leaning was towards an acer because they are the first to come in spring and the last to go in autumn. And there is a lot to be said for that. Now, I know that they too are delicate ladies and love sheltered corners, which my garden is – or least so I thought until the recent catastrophe, which was hopefully a once-in-a-lifetime occurrence. Now, acers come in many shades, heights and sizes, and getting the right one would be the challenge. But what a delightful challenge! The Acer Palmatum Sango-Kaku seemed to have everything I needed in a tree. Then the idea of a Gleditsia Sunburst came into my head. Though not as beautiful as the frisia, she is not as fragile either. Replacing Uncle Jacky's apple tree was going to be interesting. On occasions such as this, Brendan Kennelly's poem 'Begin' always comes to mind: showing that no matter what the circumstances, there is inbuilt within each one of us the irrepressible urge to begin again.

Begin

Begin again to the summoning birds
to the sight of the light at the window,
begin to the roar of morning traffic …
… Begin to the loneliness that cannot end
since it perhaps is what makes us begin,
begin to wonder at unknown faces
at crying birds in the sudden rain
at branches stark in the willing sunlight
at seagulls foraging for bread
at couples sharing a sunny secret
alone together while making good.
Though we live in a world that dreams of ending
that always seems about to give in
something that will not acknowledge conclusion
insists that we forever begin.

Brendan Kennelly

4

The Aga and Me

Some things in life throw you way off balance. When my Aga is out of kilter I'm out of kilter. For this there is no rational explanation because when this happens my state of mind is simply beyond human logic. There is a very complex relationship between a woman and her Aga. It is an unorthodox relationship which can only be understood by another female Aga owner. The male of the species seems to be totally at sea in the midst of this female malaise and totally perplexed and bewildered when their normally capable female household companion is suddenly incapacitated, and totally banjaxed by the antics of her Aga-in-trouble.

But to put this complex situation in context, an explanation of historical Aga lineage needs to be told. As with so many things in life, it is all in the story. To the non-Aga owner, an Aga is just a cooker. But not so, not so! To an Aga owner her Aga is a much-loved, treasured member of the family. It sits in the corner of her kitchen emitting a soothing, all-embracing warmth which when you return from the upheavals of outside life reaches out and wraps you in its all-encompassing, motherly embrace. It assures you that no matter what is going on outside, all is well within. Needless to mention, one can only think of the Aga in the female format because her maternal warmth is comparable only to the bosom of an ever-welcoming, loving Nana. When outside temperatures are at zero, the Aga pours forth her warm, loving kindness all over the kitchen and surrounding rooms and if you are in need of an infusion of extra comfort you can open her top door and strategically place your lower regions in front of her, and a gush of warmth zooms up and down through all your chilly zones, akin to an infusion of a soothing tranquilliser.

This same hot top oven is ever ready to bake, roast or grill without preamble and her lower, simmering companion is on constant standby to keep all kinds of meals warm for latecomers to the kitchen table. Both ovens ooze a warmth into adjoining built-in cupboards where outdoor boots and socks absorb a steady heat and are ever-ready to give an embracing warmth to all seeking wrap-around comfort. A rack above her head and a rail along her front gently emit deep heat, infusing in-depth drying into rain-sodden outdoor wear. Her top hot plate is on constant standby to whirl a large morning kettle into jigtime singing and later has the ability to spread out her arms around a multiplicity of dinner pots, while her cooler twin companion plate simmers and soothes at a more even pace. She it is who gushes hot water from taps all over the house and renders a visit to a nearby linen room or hot press an unbelievably pleasurable warm embrace. The Aga, no matter what her age – and she is age-less – is the heart of the home and has an unexplainable deep-pitted relationship with the woman of that house. This is not a flash-in-the-pan mad love affair, but a deep-rooted liaison forged over many years of constant dependability, during which the Aga is as constant as the Northern Star. This relationship lies outside the male conceptual zones, and convinces male sufferers that when the Aga is out of action his partner-in-life has lost the plot and could very easily, despite a long and stable marital relationship, dispense with his presence in her life more readily than that of her Aga.

Sometimes the seeds of this love affair with an Aga has historical roots. Mine goes back to my school days. We did not have an Aga in our house and if we had I would have missed out on the experiences of growing up with an open fire, which was the dying gasp of a departing way of life that I am glad to have experienced. But neighbours, who were also cousins, had one. When we moved on from going to national school through the fields we graduated to a secondary school in the nearby town. This involved a three-mile morning walk, and *en route* we called to our neighbours' house where we were joined on our journey to school by cousins of the same age. It was in this house that I first came across an Aga.

Up on those high hills of North Cork along the Cork-Kerry border, winters come with a frosty face. On those mornings when we braced ourselves against the harsh cold, a break from the Arctic conditions was very welcome. In their warm house we gathered around the Aga and thawed our frozen fingers along its warm top, and then massaged our chilled bottoms across the Aga's warm, comforting front. On those freezing winter mornings, she was a huge comfort zone on our chilly journey to school.

My next encounter with an Aga was when, having completed my term in that local secondary school, my mother deemed it necessary that I spend a year in a school of domestic science with the Drishane nuns before I was launched into the working world. Known as the Sisters of Saint Theresa of the Child Jesus, this order of nuns, with French origins, also had an attached boarding school where they were more intent on turning out well-rounded, well-polished citizens than academic achievers. But most of us in their domestic science school had already gone through secondary school, so this year for us was a bit like the Transition Year in modern schools. It was a breather before stepping into the working world.

I loved my year there. We floated between the sewing, laundry, house-craft rooms and the kitchen. And in this kitchen I had my second life-enhancing encounter with an Aga. At the end of a long corridor on the wall right opposite the door into a large, roomy, quarry-tiled kitchen sat a magnificent four-oven Aga. She turned this huge kitchen, teeming with teenage cooking activity, into a warm, welcoming hub. We all loved the Aga, which overnight gently cooked our large pot of porridge and on Sunday mornings turned out trays of golden sausages. She oozed warmth all over that end of the school. I came away from Drishane with a vague intention that somewhere in my future life an Aga might feature. However, my first domestic nest was a very small house attached to a village shop where the kitchen was not much larger than an Aga. But all things come to those who wait and some years later a large, rambling house next door came on the market and my husband and I bought it and turned it into a guest house. My Aga hour had come at last!

The road to my final Aga acquisition was strewn with growling bank managers and demanding Bord Fáilte officials, but eventually a light appeared at the end of a long financial tunnel and when the time came to lay out the kitchen, my longterm dream of an Aga swam to the fore. Back in 1966 a firm called Campbell and Cook were the Aga handlers and after much toing and froing and discussion of chimney vents and draughting, a grand man called Joe Higgins came to install the Aga. It then cost the princely sum of 130 pounds, which now may seem paltry but back then was a sizeable amount of money, especially if you were cash-strapped. Over the years Joe, a fatherly figure, became my dependable Aga man and every year I received a phone call instructing me: 'Alice, turn off the Aga, I'll be out in the morning.' And he never failed to arrive and do a super job and never lost his cool even when during one particularly long Aga overhaul one of my toddlers poured a bottle of washing-up liquid into his tool box. Joe calmly moved the offender to a safe distance and patiently proceeded to wash his sudsy tools. He had the patience of Job. But, as with all of us, the frailties of old age caught up with Joe and he could no longer service Agas, which is a physically demanding job. So Joe called it a day.

By then many women in our long-tailed family had become Aga owners so one enterprising husband, who is blessed with a skilful pair of hands and a brain to match, decided to tackle the job and has succeeded in keeping our many Agas purring contentedly for years. I sometimes think – and without any rational explanation – that the reason that Paddy has succeeded so well with his Aga maintenance is because he is also into horses and horse breeding. Now, you may well ask where is the connection between a well-bred horse and an Aga? Well, a horse is a big strong powerful animal but mentally is as finely tuned and as difficult to master as a delicate violin. Ask any trainer or jockey. Likewise, the Aga, which when you see her being serviced you marvel at her large, heavy inner parts, but still when it comes down to finally getting her perfectly tuned to execute a top-rate performance, she is as delicate to tune as a Stradivarius. Both horse and Aga require strength and expert sensitive handling to achieve a perfect result. Even the best horse trainer knows that when his horse is seriously out of order and not producing the desired results he needs to call in a vet. Likewise with my Aga, when, before Christmas this year, she went seriously out of kilter, and so did my state of mind. Paddy tried everything, but she would not play ball and sat in the corner refusing to heat up. However, she still grudgingly boiled the kettle and slowly cooked meals and was still producing enough hot water for showers. But she was not in her usual form and one morning, as soon as I opened the kitchen door, I knew that she had abandoned ship. She had given up the ghost. It was time to call in an expert!

In the horse world they have the Horse Whisperer who can get into the head of a horse. In the Aga world, Paddy's friend Donal is the equivalent. He was reared with an Aga-loving mother and totally understands their complicated balance. And so he came early one morning and spent the whole day gently operating on the innards of my Aga. He was like a surgeon doing open-heart surgery. In the patience department he was in a league all his own. Maybe the fact that he had taught teenagers for many years and was thus exposed to the ups and downs of teenage tantrums, had helped cultivate this serenity. He brought to mind the value of the words: 'If you can hold your head when all about you are losing theirs ...' because undoubtedly, with my Aga appearing to lose her fight for life, I was on the verge of losing my reason.

And that evening, after a day spent trying to fix it, when Donal told me that he would need to order a new control box I swallowed hard and asked, 'How long will that take?' 'I'll order it in the morning and it should be here the day

after – but as soon as it comes I'll be right back,' he told me sympathetically. However, we had not anticipated the pre-Christmas post frenzy when the courier and postal services went bananas. So the new part failed to arrive as planned, and the Aga and I lived together in mutinous frozen silence. No heat, no cooking facilities and no hot water. The house got colder and colder, and I kept warm by going for long walks and venting my frustration on all willing or even unwilling to listen. The only people who really understood my dilemma were fellow female Aga owners. But Donal was not to be deterred by the failed delivery and he unearthed an old control box, reconditioned it and arrived early one morning and installed it, cautioning: 'This could be fine, but facing into Christmas with a turkey and ham on the horizon, I'd be happier with the new one. As soon as it comes I'll be back to install it.' At that point I felt like going down on my knees in thanksgiving to this patient, obliging man who was going above and beyond the call of human kindness in coming to install this temporary measure until the new box arrived. Like everyone else in the weeks prior to Christmas he was rushed off his feet. But when I endeavoured to thank him, he smiled understandingly saying, 'When we were young and our Aga was in trouble, so was my mother.' So I was dealing with a man who understood! Many years ago there was an English women's magazine called *Woman's Weekly* which ran a weekly column called 'The Man Who Knows'. Here was such a man.

The Aga slowly and grudgingly came back to life, but remained lethargic, and I found myself constantly testing her temperature like a doctor with a dodgy patient. So I was delighted when a few days later Donal rang to say that the new control box had arrived and he was coming the following morning to install it. With the installation of her new control box, my Aga hummed back into action and when, the morning after her heart surgery, the kettle danced off her hot plate once again, I knew that her transplant was a complete success. Warm house, cooking facilities and showers were once again mine. The Aga was back in full stride and so was I.

5

Older, But Not Wiser

Last October I did a poetry reading at a local Arts Festival. I had promised to do this for the previous two years but had had to cancel, the first year due to the fact that my daughter had a surprise holiday booked for the same date, and on the second occasion due to being laid low with Covid. So, this third time round I was paranoid that something would prevent me being there, which I really did not want as the organisers had been so understanding and kind on the two previous occasions. I felt that I just could not let them down for a third time. Also, I felt that the inability to do what I had promised to do would seriously dent my self-belief. But I got there, much to my relief, and all went well.

Still, on returning home I began to ask myself some questions. Maybe having too many commitments lined up might not be such a bright idea? Maybe I hadn't taken this need to slow down seriously enough?

Amongst other commitments there was one other such occasion already promised that I also really wanted to do and this was the launching of a book in the Bon Secours Hospital in Cork (The Bons) which was scheduled for the 18 December. But before that event there were a few other big occasions on the horizon and though all were pleasant experiences it was good to have them behind me. And then Christmas was on the horizon, but before Santa could come down my chimney the summer window boxes had to be replaced by the spring ones because I always feel that we really need flowers in the bleak days of January and February. That done, the yard and garden had to be put to bed for the winter. Then it was time to put up the Christmas tree with the help of my granddaughter Ellie, who lives nearby. She loved every minute of it because when you are twelve years old Christmas decorating is a delightful exercise. As we took some ancient, fragile decorations out of their boxes I told her all their stories, which she loved. And when we were finished and stood back to admire our efforts, she requested earnestly, 'Nana, will you leave all your Christmas decorations to me?' Don't you love the honesty of children? And it was lovely to see how much she appreciated the old decorations and their stories.

We were both delighted to have the house ready for Christmas. The mincemeat for the mince pies was also in readiness, with plans that Ellie and her two little brothers would come and help with a big bake-up on the Sunday before Christmas.

But during all this time I had an uneasy feeling that my internal engine was slightly out of order. Sometimes it felt as if I was driving up a steep hill with the brakes on. However, I hoped that by driving on, things might sort themselves out. How stupid can you get? But I always have a problem with differentiating between what is the natural progression of years and a curable health complaint. Also, at the back of my mind, I worried that I might not be able to make it into the Bons hospital to do the book launch on the night of 18 December. This was a book launch that I really wanted to do because I had been involved in the preparation of the book, which had been a work in progress for a few years. I also felt I owed a debt of gratitude to the Bons going back over many years. Even before I was born, my mother had been very ill there for over six weeks, during which time my father, despite having three small children to mind and a farm to run, made the journey many times. The journey to Cork from the Cork-Kerry border in the early thirties was like going to America in today's world. And years afterwards, when all was well, if you mentioned the Bons in conversation Dad would enquire, 'Is that man with the sword still half-ways up the stairs in there?' He was referring to St Michael, the Archangel, pinning the devil to the ground with his sword.

Then, some years later, my little brother Connie died in the Bons, and my mother was very grateful to the nuns and the young Dr Kevin Kearney who cared for him there.

Many years later I met up with the same Dr Kearney who looked after one of my children after he had a bad accident. And over the years, like a lot of Cork families, we had various bits and pieces removed and replaced in the Bons.

Then a few years ago the senior nurses in the Bons who were the first lay staff to be trained by the nuns, felt that before their own retirement they should in some way acknowledge the great training that these nuns had passed on to them. Many of these nuns were now gone, but some quite elderly nuns were still living in an adjacent convent. The publication of this book, *Values from the Ground Up*, would also mark the arrival of the order in Cork two hundred years earlier in

1824 to set up this hospital. So, the idea of a book as a fitting tribute came about. After much discussion it was decided that each nurse would write about the nun who had trained her, thus covering all the different departments in the hospital, the wheels of which are still oiled by the dedicated training of those nuns. It was fascinating to read the memories of these now-mature nurses as they looked back at the lighthearted, irresponsible trainees that the nuns had moulded into the capable nurses they are today. My contribution to this book was to write a foreword and do the launch. The first was accomplished but the latter was yet to be done.

Despite having some dodgy days I convinced myself that all would be right on the night. That, however, was wishful

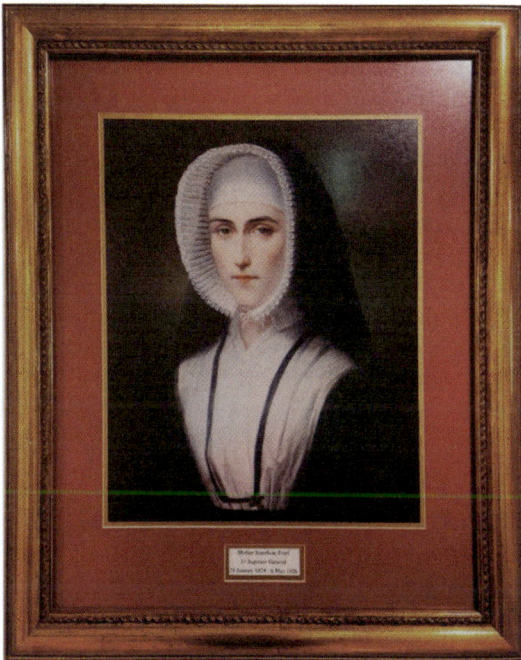

thinking and eventually I had to give in and make my way down to Dr Máire who runs a super clinic down our street, with Dr Fiona and Nurse Moira. Between the three of them they keep the parish standing.

I began by telling Dr Máire that I had to be in the Bons that night to do a book launch, but after a quick health check she informed me: 'Oh, you'll be in the Bons tonight all right, but in your pyjamas.' And that is exactly what happened. But before getting to the pyjama stage in the Bons there was a bit of a detour. First into the Assessment Department where I got what you could only describe as a body NCT, the result of which deemed that this body was not road-worthy. But before I was dispatched to the repair unit upstairs, I had a question for the consultant in charge of the Assessment Department: 'Would it be all right if I went across the corridor to the restaurant, now, to do a book launch?' He was somewhat taken aback and demanded, 'Do you feel able?' 'I do,' I assured him, though not quite sure if that was really the case. 'Highly unorthodox,' he informed me, 'but a nurse will accompany you and you're to leave when she beckons.'

Normally if you are given the honour of doing a book launch or even attending one you dress up and look good for the occasion, so I knew that all the people there would be in their best bib and tucker. The place was decorated like a Christmas wonderland for the occasion. I was still in the woolly jumper and baggy pants in which I had come in earlier, and after all the overhauling in the Assessment

Department was a bit bedraggled-looking, and far from the image one would wish to have for a book launch. However, this was no time for vanity and I was very grateful to be able to do the launch, which I did to the best of my ability, and when my *aide de camp* nurse beckoned, I obeyed. Job done!

Normally I do not like being in hospital. Who does? But on this occasion common sense prevailed with the realisation that this was the best place to be and that the time had come to go with the medical flow. I had brought with me a selection of books because you never know until you are in hospital what book will best suit. The one that hit the spot on this occasion was John Creedon's *This Boy's Heart*, which made me smile through all the pages. The view from my window was very pleasant. Right out front was a large Christmas tree and across the road some fine old houses had a festive glow. The whole hospital was beautifully decorated for Christmas and the chapel glowed in candlelight and floral arrangements. Each morning, Mass was accompanied by the wonderful singing of a member of the Pastoral Care Team. Here they care for body and soul. One day along a wide corridor there was a Christmas market and it was good to see the amazing range of handmade gifts and homemade products available. Another day a group of elegant ladies gave a wonderful musical recital at the end of a wide corridor for the entertainment of patients, visitors and staff.

The medical care was meticulous, and the food was superb, and with each day I began to feel better. It was very interesting to see and experience the superb training as described in their book still being carried on in the Bons today. And Yes, my father's 'man with his sword' is still half-way up the stairs.

But it was wonderful to be home for Christmas. Had I learnt anything about the need to heed the warning signs of an approaching storms? That's a work in progress!

6

Candlemas Day

Yesterday was Candlemas Day, 2 February. After weeks of freezing and stormy conditions, this beautiful warm day arrived, full of sunshine and soft breezes. My mother used to call such a day a 'pet day', maybe after the pet animals that were then a frequent part of farm life. The pet lamb or the pet calf were fragile and delicate, and needed to be minded and nurtured because they might not last long. And yesterday was such a day. A day to be loved, absorbed and appreciated because it was a temporary solace between what had gone before and could come again.

But apart from the day itself I love the sound of the word 'Candlemas' as it has an Old World quality. Some words bring certain images to mind and with Candlemas come pictures of candles and sconces – and if you never heard of a sconce ask your Nana. Candlemas also brings to mind tall,

elegant, flickering candelabra full of church candles that had to be put out with a special long-handled candle quencher. By a strange coincidence, a beautiful picture of candelabra arrived yesterday by email from John Scally, who lectures in Trinity College and sends out spiritually uplifting messages at the beginning of each month. His email highlighted the story that Candlemas celebrates the day when Mary and Joseph brought the Child Jesus to the temple where Anna and Simeon were delighted to welcome them.

My father had his own explanation for the significance of Candlemas day in rural living. He told us that from Candlemas onwards the candles, which up to that date were lit all around the house, were then no longer considered necessary and were put away to be lit again months later when shorter days came about. This was a major event. And that was also the era of waste-not, want-not. From Candlemas onwards people worked only with natural daylight. They got up with the morning light and stopped work when it faded. And, as if in keeping with his long memory of that tradition, my father died on Candlemas Day. His going was as gentle as the blowing out of a candle, so yesterday, to remember him and celebrate Candlemas, I lit a candle on my kitchen table, a pure wax candle, the flame of which was a steady golden orb. To sit in silence and be absorbed into its mellow depths as it filled the kitchen with its delicate honeyed smell was to be encompassed into a calm, remembering, meditative time.

Maybe one of the blessings to balance the slowing down of ageing is that now you take the time to savour such moments; time to absorb and appreciate little things that previously you ran past as there was so much that had to be done. So, this morning when I woke up too late to get myself up the hill at a comfortable pace in time for our Monday morning Mass, I decided instead to stay put and enjoy whatever alternatives evolved. Here in Innishannon we are lucky enough to still have weekday mass on Monday and Wednesday mornings. The light of early morning when you step out the door brings you alive, and going up the hill to our church in the morning is an invigorating experience. The hill is alive with children going up to the school, which is just beyond the church, and cars are filing in and out of the conveniently placed church car park. Outside noise does not penetrate through old church walls, so after the pandemonium on the hill the church is an oasis of peace and tranquility. Early comers have candles already lit on the candelabra by the altar.

But this morning because I did not wake up in time, I did not make it to Mass as rushing up steep hills is now off my agenda. However, dawdling in bed is not good for the body or mind, so I got myself onto the floor and knelt to say some morning prayers. For some strange reason I am not a night-prayer person. Maybe I feel that once in bed there is not much to go wrong other than I might not wake up there the following morning. But how bad would that be? Sometimes, however, I wonder might it be good for me to resume the practice when the saying of an old neighbour farmer comes to mind; as he knelt would tell us 'Even the cows kneel at night.' This was a man of the land who loved his cows. And my grandmother's lengthy night prayers consisted of a flurry of rosaries and countless other invocations, but as her final night prayer she would say the simple, child-like prayer: 'Matthew, Mark, Luke and John, bless the bed that I lie on, and if I die before I wake, my soul I give the Lord to take.' It was as if she was signing herself off day duty and putting the Lord on night duty. But mornings are different and then I feel the need to get all my ducks in a row before facing into the day. And sometimes I use a kneeling cushion because it was a gift from a good friend and brings many blessings into my days. It exudes a feel-good sense. So, after asking the 'man himself' to take care of the day, I round up my A Team, consisting of all my dearly departed who, I feel, have the time and a certain responsibility to look after those they have left behind!

Then, this morning, I made my way across the room to view the outside window-box. The happy yellow and orange primroses are a joy to behold, as are the tête-à-tête daffodils that are strutting their stuff above them. I eased open the window to remove a few yellowing primrose leaves that might spread their mould to the others. Spring flowers are stepping stones into brighter days.

Breakfast over, I made a snap decision to hose down the stepping-stones along the garden paths. These large, flat stones were salvaged years ago from an old house being taken down across the road. They now make the paths of the garden more interesting and a pleasure to walk on.

Sometimes, however, these stones need to have their faces washed. And what a variety of interesting faces they have: moon-shaped, oval-shaped, long-faced, sharp-faced, kindly-faced, they all have their own story to tell. And then came a different one. As the lichen and moss eased off this stone, writing began to come to the surface. And then slowly a memory twig began to flutter at the back of my brain. Back in 2016 when we held our first Gardens and Galleries event, my friend Jane and her sister had brought the gift of a stone plaque which was then laid on the garden path. But the intervening years had totally obliterated it and now here it was coming to life to tell its story once again: 'Old Gardeners Don't Die, They just Spade Away' it said. How true!

Later that evening I walked slowly up to the church to light a candle in celebration of my father and Candlemas Day.

7

The Young Ones

'It's a baby girl!' The midwife's pronouncement seeped into my befuddled brain igniting a tiny spark of joy that quickly suffused my entire being. At last, after four boys, a girl! I had hardly dared to hope for this, and my mother had sensibly silenced any such voiced wishes with the declaration that a healthy baby was the end aim of this game. And, of course, she was right. But Aunty Peg, who lived next door and shared our lives, would sometimes say wistfully, as she watched our four little boys whom she dearly loved at play, 'Wouldn't it be great if we had a little girl.' And on the evening of the First Holy Communion Day of the youngest lad I felt a certain sad pull at my heartstrings that this was the last Holy Communion day to be celebrated in our house. Those were lovely togetherness days which we all enjoyed, days when my parents and family members travelled from North Cork, and Uncle Jacky and Aunty Peg and local cousins joined us around the kitchen table in celebration. And afterwards we all rambled out into the garden to take pictures under Uncle Jacky's apple tree.

That Saturday night as I tidied up after the youngest lad's First Holy Communion, I felt a certain sense of regret that this kind of gathering was now over for us. But I was reckoning without Aunty Peg! Soon after that Communion day she departed for heavenly heights and what she had wished for on earthly pastures she achieved from higher zones, and within a year of her departure I was being told in the Bons: 'It's a girl.' My mother used to proclaim that when 'prayers went up, blessings came down'. But Aunty Peg went up herself and made sure that blessings came down.

In appreciation of the great women who had gone before our daughter, we gave the new baby Aunty Peg's and her two grandmothers' names, which caused one of my friends to comment: 'There is a great air of finality about this christening with all the ancestral women lined up.' As a child I had never liked my 'ancestral' name, but in later years I appreciated the wisdom of the handy neighbour who, having delivered me, pronounced that a continuation of an old family name, such as Alice, enriches the child and strengthens their connection to the family tree.

So this new baby girl entered our mostly male household and learned quickly, with the help of cousin Con who lived with us, how to hold her ground against 'the brothers', as she termed them. Her father's one disappointment was that she showed no interest in mastering his violin and concertina but opted instead for the world of horses, which would have proved a challenge but for the help of a Sweetnam cousin who lived outside the village. Having finished college, she, like so many of her fellow students, headed for America, and I wondered if she would meet a dashing Yank or other nationality who would sweep her off her feet. But thankfully she opted for a North Cork man and returned home to live in a house just up the hill.

During the restoration of their house she and her husband moved in with me and when their first baby arrived she spent her first few months here. By then I was on my own and it was great to have a baby in the house with her baby smells, coos and cuddles, but also good that when she cried at night I could roll over and go back to sleep glad that I was not the one on night feeds!

By then I already had three older grandchildren but was very conscious of the Mary Kenny caution that 'A mother-in-law's place is in the wrong.' However, with a daughter one felt freer to offer advice and to be more involved. As little Ellie grew, it was a great joy to share the new parents' delight and excitement in all she did and to witness this baby's first hesitant steps.

Baby Strides
First steps,
Delighted face.
She no longer

Views the world
From below up,
But looks at life
Straight in the eye.

Living so close to them was a real blessing but I constantly kept in mind the Mary Kenny caution, regularly
reminding myself that no man wants to see his mother-
in-law in situ every time he walks in his front door. After
a few years Ellie was joined by two brothers and theirs
became a hectic household with both parents working and the usual mad scramble to fit in training, games
and all kinds of non-stop activities. Often a phone call
comes asking, 'Mam, are you busy?' or 'Mam, what are
you doing tonight?' And I am glad to be available. And
often when they are walking to the nearby playground
or sports pitch they wave when passing by or come tum-
bling in the door.

Gaggle of Golden Goslings
Watering the window boxes,
When across our busy road
Cascading through non-stop traffic
Comes a waterfall of happy voices,
'Nana' in an exuberant holler.
They wait, waving impatiently
For the red man to go green,
While beaming Baby Conor

Rocks his buggy with delight.
When the green man flashes
A flight of golden goslings
In a flurry of open wings fly
Through arrested traffic
Into my waiting arms.

A gorgeous moment
To be forever treasured.

Ellie comes after school one day a week and Tim another day, and Conor will probably be next in line. They can be so amusing. Conor is into forthright pronouncements and recently on receiving an injection in our local clinic accused the nurse in a shocked voice: 'You made a hole in me.'

One of Ellie's favourite pursuits is baking and she has now mastered the making of an 'Aunty Peg apple cake', very traditional in our family, and is a dinger at peeling apples, which is my least favourite part of the job. She is also into more adventurous baking pursuits, but instead of resorting to a cookbook, the internet is invoked, which is beyond my digital expertise, and instead of watching the clock or using a timer, Echo is instructed to do the timing, which I find totally mesmerising. All this plunges me into a new world totally beyond my comprehension. However, when the season is right, Ellie is also into blackberry picking and in this we are joined by Tim. Tim, however, has far less challenging pursuits as he enjoys feeding the birds and meandering around the village. During Covid they regularly stood on the street outside my window and entertained me while I remained locked up inside. This happened so often that I think Tim, who was about four at the time, must have decided that I belonged in a locked-away situation because the first time that I appeared outside their window he put his head out and demanded, 'Nana, who let you out?'

Amongst their many activities they have discovered with the help of our brilliant local school and Comhaltas Ceoltóirí Éireann the magic of music and have mastered the tin whistle and the concertina, and their grandfather's violin has finally come out of its old case. I love to hear them play, knowing the joy it would have brought to Gabriel to hear his much-loved instruments back in action in the hands of his grandchildren. He had also been a sports enthusiast and so is his son-in-law, and I often smile to see history repeat itself with non-stop dedication to training, coaching and travelling to matches all over the country. The children are all into hurling, football, soccer, rugby and athletics, which leads to crazy scheduling.

When they come down the hill to visit me the house vibrates with their young life, and when they depart I sometimes breathe a sigh of relief. As my daughter tells me: 'People love to see us come and people love to see us go.' Their house is action-packed which I find stimulates me out of the sense of detachment from life that can some-times accompany living alone. With children there is no such thing as standing on the sideline as they are into a life of non-stop action. Their enthusiasm is contagious and I get dragged into activities that I sometimes feel are beyond my capabilities, but age is no barrier to children and they see no reason why I cannot play soccer, dance to their music or run up the hill as fast as they can. Although one day when I was failing to keep up, Tim came back, took my hand and told me, 'I know that Nanas can't run fast.' I can now see the wisdom of my old friend Mrs C, who, many years ago when she moved into our then hectic house, told me: 'The old should surround themselves with the young.' But I also remember her cautionary words that 'There is nothing more boring than stories about other people's grandchildren.' What a wise old bird she was! So I have been slightly wary of writing this chapter! She handled her old age with vigour and determination, cautioning me 'If you put up with too much you get too much to put up with.'

My grandchildren sometimes come to Mass with me and Ellie enjoys being a reader and altar server, and Tim takes carrying up the gifts at Mass very seriously. When out walking and we pass our church they love to go in and light candles and then we pray for people they know who are in difficult situations, especially a friend of their father's who had a very bad accident at work and is now in a wheelchair. On these occasions we also remember the children who are suffering in war zones all over the world. Outside the church they like to visit the family grave and I get asked many question about the ancestors resting there. And it is great when First Communion days came around to once

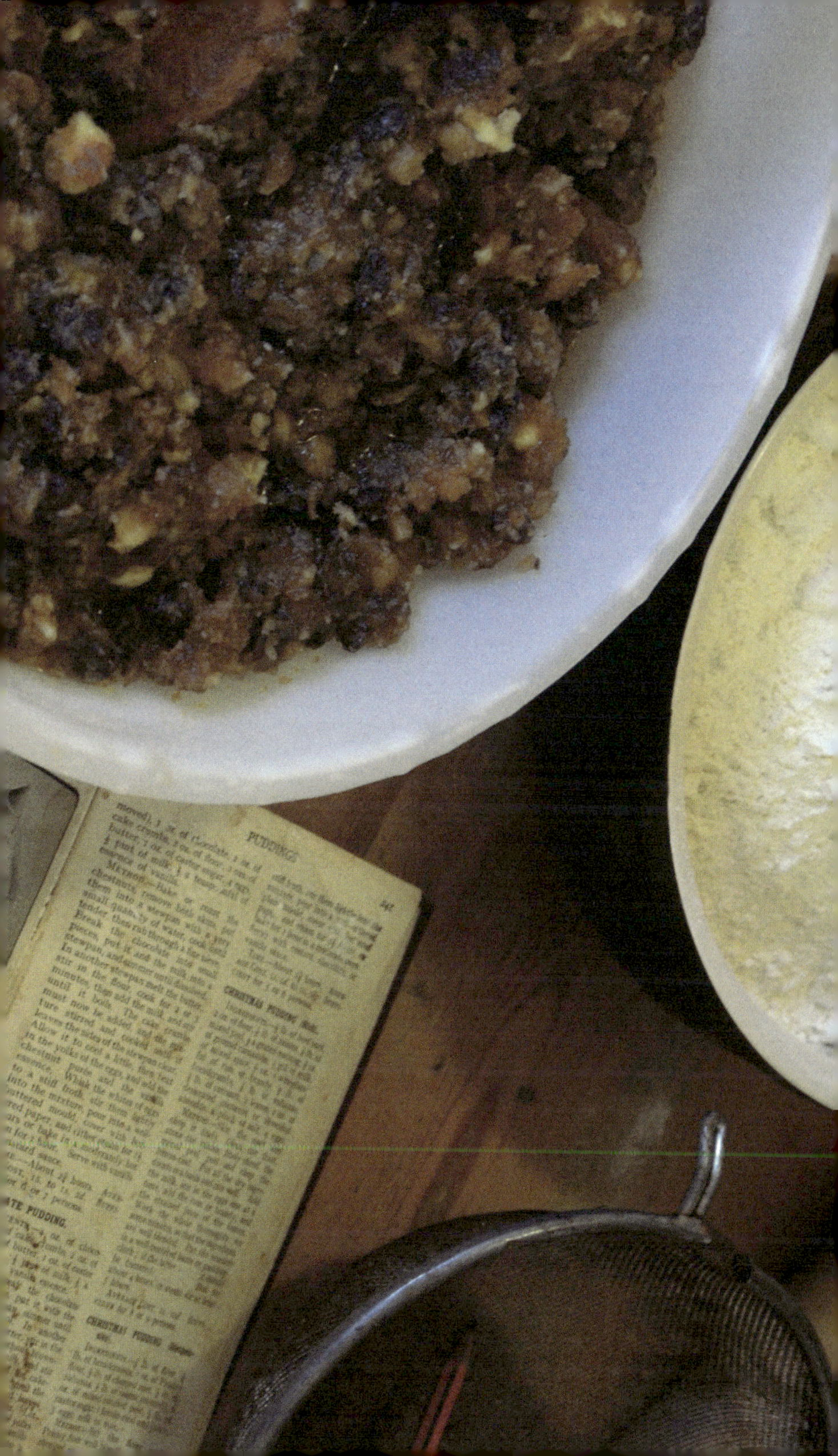
PUDDING

again enjoy the family gatherings when the extended family still travel from North Cork.

Sometimes I have dinner up in their house and like all of today's young ones they are into pastas and rice, whereas I am a roast meat, spuds and veg woman, which the children term: 'A Nana dinner.' And at Christmas they all gather in my house for a giant Nana dinner that entails all the traditional trimmings, which, now that they are getting older, they help to prepare. And the leftovers of this dinner keep us all fed for days, which leads to a total clock off from all culinary activities in both houses. I love these lazy days between Christmas and Little Christmas, which take me back to the time between the Christmases on the home farm when the land rested and so did the people. During these days the Santa gifts travel up and down the hill between the two houses.

But in the days prior to Christmas the big baking project is the making of the mince pies for which the three of them gather, with Ellie directing operations. On this occasion you need the expertise of a skilful EU negotiator to avoid a World War Three confrontation. And when the mince pies finally make it out of the Aga oven without a mishap, I breathe a deep sigh of relief. While all this baking is taking place downstairs, 'Santa' is hiding away up in the attic.

For several weeks before Christmas, we have, over the years, visited Santa in different locations. The one that I loved most, as did the children, was the one in which as we all waited with baited breath as we listened to Santa actually rumbling down a gaping chimney. First a giant red boot appeared and then, accompanied by much huffing and puffing, the rest of him slowly emerged and finally, with a warm, welcoming smile on his face he beamed out at us from a huge black fireplace. It was magic! That Christmas night I almost expected to hear him rumbling down my own chimney.

Bearing in mind Mrs C's proclamation that there is nothing more boring than stories about other people's grandchildren, I apologise if you yawned your way though this chapter!

8

Weathering Storms

Here I am in the cardiology ward of the Bon Secours hospital in Cork with two heart monitors hanging off me like a pony's tackle, and it is most intriguing that somewhere in the upper regions of the Bons my heartbeat is being monitored on a screen. The miracle of modern medicine is simply mind-boggling. I am waiting for the installation of a pacemaker. I'm a bit intrigued about this procedure as pacing myself was never one of my strong points, so I am now wondering what this pacemaker will DO for me. The installation was supposed to be done at lunchtime yesterday and I was tested, fasted, gowned up and ready for the road, but then it got postponed due to an emergency coming into the operating theatre. So this morning I am on standby and awaiting the arrival of the cardiologist to fill me in on his plan. So, somewhat like Beckett, I am waiting for Godot.

In the medical world, consultants are the gods who call the shots.

But thankfully the Cheltenham races are on at the moment so I watched them on the TV yesterday, and the plan is if confined to barracks again today to do the same. There is nothing like horse-racing to bring the outdoors indoors. And thankfully, outside a window at the end of an adjacent corridor is the blessing of a magnificently aged magnolia tree, which is slowly coming into bloom. I regularly walk along the corridor and the sight of some more blossoms having arrived on the tree is uplifting and strangely comforting. I have always been fascinated by the breathtaking beauty of mature magnolia trees. They may only bloom for a short time, but if the weather is kind they can keep going for a longer period and their beauty is food for the soul. But if stormy weather comes their beautiful blooms can disappear overnight. A bit like ourselves, they can be blown away! But this great old tree stands in a sheltered corner outside the window, and in addition to its gorgeous blossoms has a great curved trunk of many humps and hollows with interlaced gnarled branches reaching to the sky.

This old tree tells the story of growing old, and maybe it is advising me to do the same – to think about and tell the story of my own ageing. Is this time in the Bons my gap time to articulate the ups and downs of our later years? Maybe …

Inevitably as the years go by, repairs and maintenance become part of the ageing process and you learn that these are the handrails to help you cope with the challenges that

may accompany this time of life. With ageing, certain limitations are thrust upon us, so maintaining as good a quality of life as possible, despite the limitations that come our way, is the name of the game. And it can be a tough game. You can no longer run the length of the pitch, maybe cannot see the ball as clearly as you once did and sometimes find it difficult to hear the voices of other players and the referee! But, as my longtime friend Maureen always advised: 'We must row with the oars we have.' Maureen and I were friends and walking companions for many, many years. We had children of similar age, read and discussed the same books and had shared great times when we travelled together to many book signings and readings. So, when she died quite quickly from cancer a few years ago, her going left a huge gap in my life. And maybe this is one of the roughest aspects of growing old: you have to say goodbye to many whom you have dearly loved.

But these partings also focus your mind on the brevity of your own life, which also makes you think about the end of your own journey. And, while not looking forward to journey's end, I am hugely curious about what lies beyond. And even though sceptics declare that a belief in a hereafter is merely the opium of the people, they might be wrong. Could it be that what is beyond this world is also beyond our human understanding? And maybe that is just as well because when you look at our world and see what we human beings are doing to each other at this side of the great divide, it is probably best that we are locked out of whatever lies beyond. When death comes, church rituals are undoubtedly the structures that ease people through the trauma. We then need the support of our extended family and community and the church services provide the scaffolding for bringing all that together.

Many years ago when my brother-in-law died suddenly at a young age we were all shattered. Maybe we had thought back then that death belonged to our parents' generation but not with us young ones in our twenties. Bill was the first of our generation to die. This was a blast of reality and out of step with our perception of how things should be. What took me a little by surprise when it happened was the reaction of my father. Telling him this sad news was not going to be easy as they had been such good friends. Many Sundays after Mass my parents had called to my sister's and Bill's house where my father and Bill sat for hours chatting in the front porch overlooking the garden. And other Sundays the coming together was back on the home farm where Dad and Bill walked the fields together. Now that was all over.

But Dad, to my surprise, was quietly accepting of the news. Maybe because by then he had become accustomed to accepting death. He had buried a sibling at a young age and his youngest child at the age of four. He was a man of the land who walked in harmony with nature, and so had a natural acceptance of the inevitability of death. He farmed at a time when farming was not as it is today and animals died of old age on the farm. Maybe this created in him a quiet acceptance of his own death too: in later years, when sitting contentedly by the fire smoking his pipe, and when asked what he was doing, would answer with a wry smile, 'Waiting.'

Many years later, having walked six miles the previous day, my husband died suddenly. At the time it was devastating, but now in retrospect I can appreciate that it was probably best for him to get out before being beset by the frailties of old age which would have driven him crazy. In his younger years he had been a GAA referee, and once I had recovered from the initial shock of his death I perceived him as running off the pitch while he was still fit and able. Women, I think, are more tolerant of the fragilities of old age than men are, but maybe that is just my own perception because I was married to a man who literally believed that with good food and exercise you could keep up and running to the end, which is exactly what he did.

Of all the challenges we weather in life, grief must surely be one of the most difficult. Though when I voiced that opinion to a friend who was caught up in an acrimonious, long-running, family legal quagmire, she told me, 'At least death is a clean cut.' For her there were worse things than death. One never knows what others are enduring unless we have walked in their shoes.

We are usually first introduced to ageing and death through the passing of our grandparents, then our parents. I knew just one of my grandparents and in old age she was a force to be reckoned with right up until she finally called it a day. My mother was inflicted with a stroke, which is one of the unkindest cuts of all, but she bore it stoically. And my father went out like a soft breeze. Looking back now I realise that my first real encounter with the finality of death was at about the age of ten when our beloved old friend and neighbour, also named Bill, died suddenly. Bill was a second father to us, as, having no children of his own and living with his two elderly sisters, we became his adopted children. He came to our house every night bringing a bucket of spring water from the well which was at the foot of the hill that he came down on his way to our house. This was the era before piped water into rural homes and, once Bill had his bucket safely landed on a side-table in the kitchen, he took his own chair by the fire and began to teach us our lessons. These could go on for quite a while, but Bill never lost patience with us.

On Friday nights, with no lessons to be done, he taught us how to play cards and gave us lessons in Irish dancing, lining us up again and again with endless patience to instil in us the intricacies of the haymakers' jig. Bill was my comforter when at the age of four our little brother Connie died. I was then six and not quite sure what it was all about. But some years later, on the day of Bill's own funeral, I did know what it was all about, and climbed up to a high field overlooking his house and watched the hearse emerge slowly out of the haggard onto the boreen leading out of his farm. As I watched, a wave of desolation swept over me and a cold hard lump of pain erupted in the pit of my stomach, which years later my sister Ellen, speaking about grief, described as 'bleeding inside'. After his funeral I went to stay with his two elderly sisters to keep them company, and during those days I wandered around his haggard and cow stalls finding comfort in sitting on his cow stool, petting his donkey and sitting on the large stone on which he had rested nightly at the side of the hilly path coming down to our house. Was I learning to say goodbye and letting Bill go?

Letting go after a death is a slow process and I have found that dreams play a big part in the process for me. For a long time after my husband Gabriel died, I dreamt of looking through the doorway of our store room, which has steps leading down into the kitchen, and seeing him there, but wondering in the dream how that could be possible as he was dead, but I was still so glad to see him. Obviously I wasn't quite ready to let him go. And after our much-loved cousin Con, who had lived with us for many years, was swept away by cancer, I dreamt for a long time afterwards of him sitting in a boat at the side of a lake while I was on the shore holding a rope. And after Aunty Peg died the dream was of running up the stairs and opening the door into her bedroom and falling into emptiness.

Standing by a death bed must surely be one of the most extraordinary experiences of life. You can never be prepared for the profound effect of watching life ebb away and then the realisation that it is all over. It is as if someone goes over an invisible edge and you have no vision of where they are gone. I was twenty when I first had this experience. I was then working in West Cork, and a few of us young ones had

come together to visit an old lady who lived alone beside us and had no family. We helped her in any way we could – did her shopping and called in to her morning and evening to see if all was well. But one morning when I let myself in and went to her bedroom, I knew straight away that all was not well, and soon realised, to my dismay, that she was dying. I ran down the street to a telephone kiosk and called the local priest and doctor, who both came quickly. But having done what they deemed appropriate, they left. Luckily, another friend came and we sat with our old friend until she breathed her last. Looking back afterwards, I regretted that we were of such little comfort to this woman in her final hours because, being young and inexperienced, we had no coping skills.

Years later as Aunty Peg died, I became aware that I was standing on the brink of something beyond my understanding. And afterwards, coming down the stairs and into her little sitting room, which she had loved and cherished for so many years, the realisation hit me that she would never ever again be sitting there with her two much-loved dogs.

I would imagine that no matter how often we see it, death, like birth, is an overwhelming experience and understanding these events is surely beyond us humans. But, for me, witnessing death strengthened my belief in the hereafter.

But before we finally do get to the pearly gates, dealing with our daily challenges is a constant. And maybe one of the most sobering realities of growing old is the mental challenge of accepting the fact that we can no longer do what we always did, while at the same time not becoming totally obsessed with these limitations. The late Maeve Binchy had a wonderful approach to this: when she and her friends got together in their later years Maeve would announce, 'Now, just ten minutes for the medical, and then on to other subjects.' How wise was that? There is nothing more boring and soul-destroying than our own or other people's pills, pains and operations.

Now, some days I feel as if I'm in my mid-fifties and other days feel every day of my eighty-seven years (and sometimes I feel 187!), and on those eighty-seven-year days I find myself quoting Yeats's poem, 'A Faery Song':

> We who are old, old and gay,
> O so old!
> Thousands of years, thousands of years
> If all were told.

The faeries, of course, were different beings altogether, but maybe because I grew up beside a fairy fort, they were part of our world.

Perhaps as our bodies grow older the job of fashioning our minds to cope with this process is one of our greatest challenges. We can adopt different attitudes: the issue brings to mind Dale Carnegie's oft-quoted lines:

> Two men looked out from prison bars,
> One saw the mud, the other saw stars.

But sometimes it is not that easy to see those stars. One of my steps to those stars is the garden. The garden always injects new life into me and every morning when I go out and walk around it, it fills me with an appreciation of its many blessings: the morning light, the sight and sound of the birds and the sense that this was and still is a much-loved corner of creation. The work of the divine creator and the invisible link between the natural and the divine is out there – all totally beyond my understanding, but for which one has to be truly grateful. I am blessed in having family nearby and great neighbours, which is one of the privileges of village living. And, of course, walking is a daily lifeline, especially in the early morning when the light is best, as we are hugely affected by light. A friend now long gone constantly told me that walking releases the happy hormones, and my father walked the fields of our farm every day declaring that it was best to keep moving rather than 'rust like an old plough in the dyke'. And in a recent interview the Olympic runner Sonia O'Sullivan said that after a walk one always feels better coming back in the door than one did going out. How true that is because when you do go out you merge into harmony with nature and are also more than likely to meet someone for a chat. I love it when people stop for a chat and are sociable instead dashing past absorbed in their mobile phone. There is great wisdom in the quote from John Donne:

No man is an island,
Entire of itself;
Every man is a piece of the continent,
A part of the main.

Like many others I was once part of a busy, hectic household and sometimes dreamed of quieter times. But at first being alone, when the family members had moved on, was bit of a culture shock, though now being alone has become a way of life that I enjoy. There is something very calming about the silence of your own house and having the time and space to do whatever you feel like doing: time to meditate, read, paint, garden; and while it is good to be pleasantly engaged there are days too when it is enjoyable to simply 'poderawl' around, as my mother used to say. This word is probably a combination of English and Irish, and I feel that such words are often more descriptive than the King's English. It means being happy to just drift around simply doing nothing or maybe bits of things.

But I also love planning projects and looking forward to pleasant occasions. Tennyson must have had that in mind when he wrote his poem 'Ulysses':

How dull it is to pause, to make an end,
To rust unburnish'd, not to shine in use!
As tho' to breathe were life!

He was so right as there is nothing more mind-deadening than the feeling you have reached a cul-de-sac in life. But of course, we all have bad days and when that happens a trusted listener is a real treasure. Not a Johnny-Fix-It, because some things in life just cannot be fixed. Neither do you need a Judgemental Johnny. You simply need somebody who knows you and your circumstances well and with whom you can let off steam. An understanding, comforting, non-judgemental, silent listener is one the greatest gifts of life.

But there is nothing more energising than planning projects and anticipating the doing of something that you know you will really enjoy.

The joy of anticipation
Awaiting dreams realisation
Looking forward is the fun
Of happy things yet to come.

So maybe, at the end of the day, our state of mind as we age is as important as the state of our body.

9

A Night Out

We all need special breaks, time out from ordinary living. They lift our heart and lighten our mood. And it is even better if you have a special favourite place for these outings. In life we all need little oases of reprieve where we can go to recover our equilibrium and be encouraged to journey on. For me over the years, one of these havens of recovery has been Man Friday restaurant in Kinsale. Last Friday night, after a long absence, I returned to Man Friday. As we drove out of Innishannon I wondered if this reunion would live up to my expectations.

I was first introduced to Man Friday back in the sixties when I was knee-deep in small children, helping run a village shop and running a newly acquired extremely busy guest house. The mid-sixties were the years before the Troubles in the North began and English tourists were pouring into Ireland. These English visitors were the bulk of our business, with some staying for two weeks during which they toured Cork and Kerry. And we got to know some of the long stayers quite well.

One of these guests was Mrs Maxwell, whom I have good reason to remember with great appreciation. She dressed impeccably, always appearing in the dining room as if she had just stepped out of the pages of a *Vogue* magazine. One morning, when all the guests had gone, she returned to the dining room where we were busy stacking plates and asked gently, 'Alice, can I have a quick word?' 'Of course,' I said, wondering what the problem was, because this was usually the reason why somebody requested 'a quick word'. But, happily, she had pleasant things in mind, a little piece of advice.

'My dear,' she asked, 'have you ever been to Man Friday?' She saw my bemused look as the only Man Friday that I had ever encountered was between the pages of *Robinson Crusoe*. She quickly enlightened me: 'It is an amazing restaurant just down the road in Kinsale and when this summer season is over and this place has slowed down you should go and enjoy its wonderful food. You will love it.' Everyone needs a treat and a break she told me. How thoughtful of her, I felt.

During that hectic summer I kept Mrs Maxwell's advice at the back of my mind, nurturing the idea of visiting this place of fine dining that had made such an impression on this woman who would only be impressed with the very best. So, at the end of the season, when all the guests had departed and life had slowed down, I planned that first visit to Man Friday. Now, I am a firm believer in the concept that you are best eating at home unless the company with whom you dine out adds to the flavour of the occasion. So, one pleasant evening, with eight chosen dining companions, my husband and I took the road to Kinsale. But because I had built up this restaurant to such a high standard for my fellow diners I was slightly apprehensive that it might not come up to expectations.

As we followed the curving road to Kinsale with its magnificent view of the river, then around Kinsale harbour, and finally climbed upwards around a wooded corner I wondered where on earth Man Friday was hiding! However, having finally found a parking space on the hill we followed our noses and then went along by a dense hedge where we spotted a discreet sign at the top of a flight of steep stone steps leading down to a partially hidden door. Man Friday was certainly not into proclaiming his presence to casual passers-by.

From the moment we went through that wooden door at the bottom of those winding steps we had a night to remember. The whole place breathed taste and elegance, and the food was absolutely divine. Seamlessly overseen by owner Peter Barry, dressed in a classy check shirt and sporting a dashing red cravat, this restaurant appeared to function with effortless ease. But, of course, that simply meant that Peter Barry was an expert at the helm. That occasion was a never-to-be-forgotten experience.

So, from that night onwards a visit to Man Friday became a rare but much appreciated treat for our family. It became the go-to place for our wedding anniversary and extra-special family occasions, and Peter Barry remained his same charming self over the years. As soon as you stepped inside its door, the stresses of the world outside simply evaporated and on a June night when my husband and I would appear, Peter never forgot that it was our wedding anniversary. My husband was a non-drinker, but I was always presented with a glass of the most wonderful wine.

Peter Barry set up the Kinsale Good Food Circle and put the town on the road to becoming the tourist mecca that it became and still is. In later years when he retired from Man Friday, it was always a pleasure to meet him on the beach in nearby Garretstown where he came daily with his beloved dog. When he died, Kinsale erected a bronze bust on the seafront in appreciation of his huge contribution to the town. A richly deserved honour.

On Peter Barry's retirement Man Friday was taken over by much younger Philip Horgan, who had also a warm, exuberant personality and continued to maintain the same exemplary standard. For our family, Man Friday remained the place to go for all special occasions.

Kinsale's location, with its fortified entrance at the mouth of a large harbour, had given it a long and varied history, with two old military forts overlooking the harbour, but when peace finally reached our shores these high forts were no longer required for defense purposes. So the high hills

above Kinsale became the sites for the homes of the merchant princes of Cork and in recent years for American millionaires and an international moneyed clientele. Fortunately for Kinsale vibrant local clubs keep the community spirit alive and over the years have managed to preserve much of its local historical heritage.

Man Friday continued for many years to be my place for soothing ruffled feathers and over the years certain items on the menu became firm favourites. Their sole on the bone brought comfort to my soul and they never failed to serve the perfect Gaelic coffee. Then, as happens in most families, life-changing events came our way and Man Friday went off my agenda for a number of years. I sort of forgot about special outings to this special place. Sometimes when the people with whom you have shared happy times in a special place are gone, there is often a reluctance to return to that place until a certain amount of healing has happened.

Then after Christmas this year during a week of freezing temperatures when we were all confined to barracks, I got a bout of cabin fever for which I felt the ideal cure would be a return to Man Friday. So, on a Monday in early January, with the roads impassable but with a thaw forecast for Friday, my daughter booked a table for four on Friday night. This was to be an all-female outing, consisting of mother, daughter, niece and daughter-in-law, four people who were comfortable in each other's company and loved to talk. The predicted thaw came on Friday morning and the whole country breathed a sigh of relief.

That night as we drove down to Kinsale I remembered my first occasion all those years ago when I had worried that I might have built up the expectations of my travelling companions to too high a level. But now it was my own expectation that I was worried about. Was I looking back at Man Friday through rose-tinted spectacles?

On entry the first surprise was that Man Friday had stretched further along the hillside, and from its new glass frontage had a breathtaking view over Kinsale Harbour, now sparkling with the lights of many yachts. And we were delighted that our table was perfectly placed to enjoy this view. We were off to a great start.

But the best was yet to come. We pored over the starters and main course and when I saw that the black sole was still on the menu I felt a glow of anticipation. My black sole and I had a wonderful reunion. Then I was tickled pink to see my old favourite crème brûlée on the dessert menu – it had made it through the years and it was still as good as I remembered! To put the final icing on the cake their Gaelic coffee came up to long-held expectations.

During the meal as the restaurant filled up around us, we enjoyed each other's company and recalled all the great nights that we had spent in this lovely place. We laughed as we remembered one night many years ago when my husband and I were heading out to celebrate our forgotten wedding anniversary, forgotten due to pressure of work. But on this particular night our then eight-year-old looked accusingly at us and moaned, 'Ye are going off out to Man

Friday while we are all here at home starving!' Over the years this story came back to tease the same eight-year-old and now the four of us, including his wife, laughed as we reminisced.

The drive home put the final magnificent touch to the evening. The road from Kinsale to Innishannon must be one of the most scenic drives in the country. This is wooded countryside through which you catch glimpses of the Bandon river through the trees. In autumn it is truly spectacular, but on a bright starry winter's night, with the moon high in the sky and the river glinting through the bare-branched trees, it is magical. It was, indeed, a night to remember. Further special evenings must be planned, I told myself. They break through the ordinariness of life in a spectacular way. Man Friday had not lost its magic touch. We would be back!

10

Gifts that Grow

E very time I walk past my thriving Peace Plant in the hallway it sparks a little ray of sunshine in my mind and puts new pep in my step. This mental uplift is beamed from the plant itself, but also by the thought of the graciousness of the people who gifted it. Over the past few summers we in Innishannon have hosted Gardens and Galleries, a celebration of our parish gardens and art galleries. The event attracts fellow gardeners and artists from surrounding parishes. When you open your garden to the public, some of the people who come in your gate can fill you with a sense of delighted surprise.

This happened to me on our very first Gardens and Galleries, when we were only beginning to find our way. A group of people walked in my gate and told us that they were from Emly Tidy Towns committee in Co Tipperary.

This is the show of support you need when you are tentatively taking the first hesitant steps on a new venture. You are wondering are you crazy, or will it work? You need a shot of assurance. And this was it.

That these people had driven all the way down from Emly to our Gardens and Galleries event was to us extraordinary, but we were to discover on subsequent encounters that these were indeed extraordinary people. Denis and Mary Heffernan and their friends have a love of their home place which has inspired them and enabled them to win the overall Tidy Towns trophy in 2009, and every other year be up there in the top awards. Denis loves Emly with a passion, but along with this is a great desire to see all other towns and villages elevate their standards. And each year since our first Gardens and Galleries, they have come from Emly to support us – and one year they made the journey even when Denis was confined to a wheelchair after a serious operation. They bring a glow of enjoyment and positivity with them, and when they leave you feel energised by their visit. Last year they came bearing the gift of a large homemade fruit cake that Mary had baked, and also a beautiful Peace Plant. Bringing peace and joy is truly their creed in life. Since then this plant has graced my front hallway, giving me great joy, but also creating an awareness that this lovely plant depends on me for its wellbeing. I was not always a good house-plant carer, but this Peace Plant has upped my game.

My awareness has spread to two Aspidistra plants passed on by a house-plant-loving sister, who gave them with detailed health-care instructions. Watering needs are regularly assessed and these plants are then gently immersed in a tin bath of rainwater behind the back door; and on soft, wet days left outside to have their faces gently washed by the falling rain. So, while the Peace Plant resides in the hall, the Aspidistras grace the deep window sills which are part of my old house. At the moment, the plant on the window of my quiet room, the *seomra ciúin*, brings the extra bonus of fronting the vibrant spring flowers in the window boxes outside. As I sit inside enjoying my lunch these add to the pleasure of the experience – maybe even to the flavour of the food.

Out around the yard and garden are gifts that continue to grow and also bring an appreciation of the giver to mind. On either side of the gate leading from the yard into the garden, two large golden ferns overflow from two stone pedestals; these were gifted by a much-loved sister who spent most of her life in Canada but came to Innishannon for her final years. I have no idea of the names of these ferns but they have the amazing bonus that they do not die off in winter but simply change colour with the seasons, from green to gold to amber. Like the giver, these ferns light up their surroundings. Thoughtful gifts create spurts of joy and plant seeds of hope that continue to grow.

Welcoming me as I walk through the gate into the garden is a large statue of St Joseph clad in moss and ivy. He had lost his home when he was evicted from a convent that was about to close, but Joseph was then given temporary asylum by the Rosminian order of priests and brothers of

Glencomeragh, Co Waterford, and then finally got permanent refuge here. Then, with her back to the high stone wall, is Foxy Mary, who was a birthday gift from my beloved Gabriel. Also, an elegant, supercilious-looking lady with a snooty look was gifted to me by an old friend when her lovely garden was about to be converted into a carpark. This reduction in status did not, however, change this lady's demeanour – she still looks down her nose at you when you walk up the path in her direction. All around the garden are plants given by friends and also garden urns that, as well as holding plants, also hold memories.

While the gifts of plants grow in the soil other gifts live on in other ways and continue to enrich life. By my bed is a blank-paged notebook made by the Cork Book Bindery, gifted by a friend who anticipated a need I didn't know I had. In the early morning hours before the world invades your mind, words can waltz in and paint images that if not captured can waft away like beautiful butterflies. In this little notebook these butterflies now leave their imprint before they take off and disappear out of mind into the clouds. Before this beauty enriched my life bits of paper were desperately sought to hold those fleeting images. But now this little friend is on constant stand-by. Also, on the floor beside my bed is a yearly gift of a large blank book, product of Muckross Book Bindery, and this is a journal in which you write to tell yourself how you are. Sounds crazy! It is. But it works.

What a blessing are these book binderies that create well-bound wonders, which on first handling convey a sense of excellence and continue to do so even in their constant use. Over the years as the copies of our local Christmas magazine *Candlelight* increased, some of us used these book binderies to bind a limited number into different volumes. We began with Kenny's Book Bindery in Galway, and then realised that nearer home was Muckross in Killarney, and finally became aware that there was one just in the road in Cork. All did a superb job and these bound volumes are now a constant joy to handle. There is a deep vein of appreciation in all us which responds and rejoices in the giftedness and creativity of others. Such gifts grow and enrich daily life.

11

A Delightful Day

As we walked between the two stone pillars into the old garden its arms encircled us in a warm embrace. Further along the pathway through the bare-branched trees you caught glimpses of an intriguing period cottage. This is the old historic Bride Park Cottage. It was the birthplace in 1825 of an Irishman, Patrick Ronayne Cleburne, who went on to become the highest ranking officer to serve in the American Civil War; it is now the home of DJ Murphy, an art collector and superb gardener, who generously opens his doors and gardens for fundraising events. Over the years this beautiful old cottage has been exquisitely decorated at Christmas and has attracted streams of visitors to enjoy its festive wonder, while also raising funds for the nearby Marymount Hospice. I visit this place in all the different seasons if I can. It is always a feast for the eye. Now in February, it's

Snowdrop Day at Bride Park Cottage, and the cancer unit at nearby Cork University Hospital (CUH) are the beneficiaries. DJ's brother succumbed to cancer in the CUH and this was DJ's way of thanking them for their care.

The woman who welcomed us in the gate had a warm and friendly smile and the air of being everyone's favourite aunt. Like ourselves, she was well wrapped-up, though thankfully the early-morning rain had cleared, and a tentative sun was trying to break through. Garden visiting in February is a dodgy business, so you go dressed for all kinds of everything. This garden slowly unfurls its secrets as you explore its sloping, curving lawns, pathways and hidden corners. Like the pages of a good book, the story unfolds as you journey through it. And all along the way snowdrops and multi-coloured hellebores sparkled along the base of mossy stone walls and danced around the gnarled trunks of old trees. The naked branches and trunks of these noble old trees tell the story of a long life and a sense that they have weathered many storms. Later in the year their ageing nobility and vulnerability will be hidden beneath gowns of different shades of green.

Then we came around a corner and there as a centrepiece in a curving lawn was a young tree with a garland of snowdrops at her feet. One can only imagine this young tree later in the year when she will have donned her spring, summer or autumn finery. Knowing DJ's gardening expertise, this has to be a rare specimen to be given such a central location. Some trees are fashion-conscious ladies and change their

outfits with the seasons. Unfortunately, we were not suffi-
ciently well informed to be able to identify this tree, but this
did not lessen our sense of enjoyment. We would find out
later. Visiting other people's gardens can be a learning curve
or simply an absorption of the sheer delight at the skills of
another.

As well as being a super gardener DJ has for many years
been a collector of intriguing garden sculptures and he has a
great collection of wonderfully aged and fascinating pieces.
I am particularly fond of garden sculptures and have several
in my own garden. I love to see what other people choose
for their gardens and how they position and surround them.
At the centre of one lawn was an enormous stone creation.
Narrow at the base it curved outwards towards the top. It
was an incredible piece and where it came from and how it
got to where was now resting was a question begging to be
asked. It was above waist high and its top edges curved down
into intriguing hollows and then rose into rough humps.
Surprisingly, from within its depths a multiplicity of spring
flowers – snowdrops and vibrant primulas – smiled up at us.
This ancient piece looked as if it had been quarried from
the bowels of the earth. Around some corners of the garden
we encountered well-weathered gentlemen and elegant
Grecian ladies, both popular in Victorian times, who had so
blended into their surroundings that sometimes you would
walk past them and need to backtrack to appreciate them.
As we journeyed on in wonder, snowdrops continued to
curve around every corner. Now to most of us a snowdrop

is a snowdrop, and but not so to snowdrop connoisseurs who can differentiate between the ordinary, the special and the very, very special. One of the women we encountered led us along a path to where a very special snowdrop with the unlikely name of Grumpy was to be seen. Apparently Grumpy was so special that he came at a very hefty sum. So a discussion on the merits of rare plants ensued and the philosophical conclusion was reached that perhaps beauty is indeed in the eye of the beholder.

One of the many delights of visiting open gardens is the total freedom to stop and confer about plants with fellow gardeners whom you may have never previously encountered. On our snowdrop day, a man approached us with a puzzled look on his face and enquired, 'Are you Gardens and Galleries?' Over the years people have looked at me with a slightly puzzled look on their face and asked: 'Should I know you?' or 'Have we met before somewhere?' or 'Are you *To School through the Fields*?' But Gardens and Galleries was a first. It caused his wife to laugh and enlighten us: 'We were up at it last year and had a great day. That minibus taking people around to all the gardens is a great idea. Are ye on this year?' We assured them that we were and after a discussion on the delights of Bride Park Cottage we parted company with the plan of seeing them in Innishannon in July. Two women overhearing our conversation told us that they were from Midleton garden club and requested dates and details of Gardens and Galleries. Gardening speaks all languages.

Gradually we made our way to the yard behind the cottage where plants were for sale, much to our delight. Our needs fulfilled, we headed for the tea counter. Having acquired tea and cake, we retraced our footsteps to the lower end of the garden where we sat at an ancient iron table sheltered beneath a plant-draped gazebo. Beside us water tumbled down into a little garden lake which was surrounded by a multiplicity of water-happy plants. The sound of the flowing water was magical, and more so the sound of the birds. As we had walked around the garden the sound of birdsong had been a background choir and now that we were seated we could see countless numbers of them sweep in and out through the trees. They filled the air with their songs. Here they had the perfect sanctuary, sharing a constant food supply with the ducks and rare breeds of hens in the nearby sheds.

As we walked out the gate we looked back, hoping that DJ would open this haven during the summer when his garden would be wearing a coat of different colours.

12

Our Boy

The plan for his coming had begun back in 2014 but he did not arrive in Innishannon until 2024. Our problem was that we had no place to put him. We knew the perfect place for him but we did not own it and acquiring ownership of land, no matter how small a plot, is a long and complicated legal procedure. But we felt he had hereditary rights as he had lived here behind that high stone wall in 1752 and we thought that he and his companions should be remembered near the place where they had once lived and where they had not been well treated. And because of those hard times, they had the right to be acknowledged and remembered. In other places around Ireland their compatriots had suffered the same neglect and hardship in similar schools, but nowhere was there any remembrance of these children, as far as we knew. So, in Innishannon we began the long saga of erecting a sculpture to the Charter School children, not only of Innishannon but of the rest of the country as well.

We were lucky to have this little corner in the village where a side road, remembered by locals as Charter School Hill, branched off the main road to West Cork. Circled around this corner in front of the high stone wall of the Old Rectory was a little plot where Tidy Towns had planted a garden years earlier. This location, perfectly placed in mid-village and fronting the spot where the original Charter School had stood, was the perfect site for our sculpture. Here it could be enjoyed by us locals and the many who drive through our village every day. Even though that hilly road out of the village had once been known as Charter School Hill, and many locals referred to 'going up Charter School', we still had no idea of the exact location of the Charter School, and many assumed that it was the Old Rectory. However, in the summer of 2000 a young American architect, named John Millar, came to Innishannon. He came because he was doing research for a book he was writing about the Charter Schools of Ireland. His interest in the Charter Schools was due to the fact that his period home in Virginia USA, which was known as Newport House, had been designed by the architect Peter Harrison. This was the same man who in 1733 had been appointed by the then Archbishop of Cashel to design the Charter Schools of Ireland. John Millar identified our original Charter School as a house behind the Old Rectory, which by then, of course, was a shadow of its former self. But John Millar's visit ignited our interest in the Charter School and a seed was planted: one day, we in Innishannon would commemorate these forgotten children who, when they left those schools, had gone back into the local community. Many were the ancestors of locals. But things take time and money!

Back in 1984 we had the foresight to set up a local Christmas magazine, *Candlelight*, with the purpose of recording local history, and over the years the money accrued from that was put aside for village projects. By 2014 two such ambitions had been achieved and next in line was a sculpture to commemorate the Charter School children. But first we had to acquire a site and the ideal one was that corner at the bottom of Charter School Hill. But before planning permission could be sought we had to know who owned the site. So we went to Michael, the man who owns the Old Rectory (the rector now serves from nearby Bandon). If Michael owned our desired site, we knew that all would be well, as since he moved into the Old Rectory Michael has been a go-to person for a multiplicity of local events. But Michael had no idea who owned our dream location. So, like Fagan, we had to think it out again.

But sometimes the wind is at your back and at the time a Bandon solicitor, Veronica Neville, happened to be a member of the County Council and had been very helpful to us in Tidy Towns, so we went to her with our problem. She unearthed the extraordinary fact that the little corner was still the property of the Frewen Estate. We were amazed.

This really was a blast from the past. In the seventeenth century Cromwell had gifted our village to one of his officers, a man called Adderley, and the Adderley family were the landlords here for generations until they went bankrupt and were bought out by the Frewen Estate in 1830. The Frewens owned Innishannon until it was decided that we wanted our own land back and afterwards many home owners bought out their freehold. But some little pockets of land must have remained unclaimed and were still the property of the Frewen Estate. One of these was the site for our sculpture. So Veronica made contact with the firm of PJ O'Driscoll who were the solicitors for the Frewen Estate. Amazingly they made contact with a Frewen, who very generously agreed to donate the site, with the request that we acknowledge their bequest on site, which we were pleased to do. We were on our way. Or so we thought. But 'The best laid schemes o' Mice an' Men / Gang aft agley.'

The previous sculpture of the Horse and Rider that we had commissioned for one end of the village had been grant-aided by West Cork Development, for which we had the matching *Candlelight* funds. Now we were ready to go again, when suddenly, due to political events, West Cork Development lost their funding and we did not have enough to go it alone. So we had to bide our time until the *Candelight* funds built up. By the end of 2023, with the publication of our fortieth edition, we had the funds to begin our sculpture project again. It was a case of 'all things come to those who wait'.

But by then Don Cronin, the artist who had created our first two village sculptures, had retired from doing large pieces and he recommended Sean MacCarthy, who had made the famous sculpture of Cork hurler Christy Ring which now graces Cork airport, as well as the Ballybunion sculpture of American president Bill Clinton, who had once played golf there. But before meeting up with Sean Mac Carthy, Mary and I (the two editors of *Candlelight*) discussed in great depth what we had in mind. We wanted this sculpture of the young Charter schoolboy to project a sense of hope and freedom, because, no matter what their situation, children have the innate ability to be happy in tough circumstances. Still, on the day that Sean and his wife Miriam, who works with him, were to come to visit, I felt quite nervous. How would we get on? Would they get what we had in mind? Would they have their own ideas? How would they react to my suggestions? It was vital for the success of this project that Sean and Miriam and I see eye-to-eye and be of one mind.

I need not have worried because Sean and Miriam were a gifted, creative couple, who listened, absorbed and discussed our concept, enhancing it with their active imaginations. It was obvious that this was a gifted twosome who creatively blended seamlessly together. When they left after an in-depth exchange of ideas, I was in a far better place. The concept of the boy had taken root and at the next meeting, when we knew that we were all on the same wavelength, Sean suggested that the next requirement was a model for our Charter schoolboy.

I had never realised that this would be part of the project and was pleasantly surprised that this was so. Sean enquired did I want him to link up with the College of Art and get somebody or did I want to get someone myself? I immediately thought that it would be nice to have somebody local, and Sean agreed. The children left the Charter School at the age of fourteen, so our boy needed to be boyish and not too small. What was required was a lean, light-limbed young lad. A lad at the end of the village immediately came to mind, but I also kept an eye out for someone else who might fit the requirements, just 'to be sure to be sure'. And then one afternoon, as the original choice walked past my window, I knew then that he was our boy. His name is Tadhg, and his parents, Michelle Rohu and Tom Sewell, run the Rohu Country Market at the end of the village. By sheer chance, his father, Tom, happened to be standing at the traffic lights across the road. I waited for him to cross and told him my story. 'Best talk to Michelle,' he smiled, which I did later, and both Michelle and Tadhg were delighted to be part of the project. The next time that Sean and Miriam visited, Tadhg and Michelle came to meet them.

Prior to this meeting I had no idea of all the pre-planning that was required for this modelling, but happily Sean and Tadhg immediately got on well and the whole measuring and photographing process went very smoothly. From the results Sean would do his first drawings. I awaited those first drawings with nervous apprehension. Would Sean capture the concept we had in mind? It seemed like a huge challenge. But when the drawings came they were magical! Sean had really got it. 'Our Boy', as we fondly called him, was on paper.

The next step was moving from drawing to actual model creation, which involved a lengthy process in the Cork Sculpture Factory. Our first sighting would be when Mary and I visited the factory. On that day I held my breath as Sean led us past all the different sections of the Sculpture Factory floor, with different works in progress. There in the last one was our Charter schoolboy. It was as if he had stepped out of the drawing. Mary and I were absolutely delighted – and, indeed, so was Sean that we were so happy with what he had created. It was a great day. So far, so good.

The next step was the bronzing, and we were truly blessed that Don Cronin, who had made our two other village sculptures, was doing the needful. We knew him well and were thus spared a lot of stress and worry. And having arrived at this stage it was time to prepare the site for the arrival of the Charter Boy. Pat and Bernard of Tidy Towns transplanted anything that was transplantable from the site to the new Linen Garden across the road, and then the entire Tidy Towns team spent a hard night clearing the remainder into Peter's trailer. Then local farmer John Keneally came with his tractor and digger and dug up and removed anything that was too heavy to shift manually. The local farming community around the village are unstinting in their support of Tidy Towns efforts. So, at last, the site was cleared and late one evening our local firm of Keohane Readymix

came and poured concrete free of charge with Peter and Vincent levelling as they poured. Once the concrete had hardened then began the meticulous preparation of making the plinth on which 'Our Boy' was to stand. Local carpenter Eamon, gifted with a great pair of hands and the ability to create perfection, turned out the ideal plinth, which was an excruciating exercise in balancing and levelling.

Sean was delighted with the plinth, which required a final delicate slanting tilt to facilitate the correct siting for his sculpture. And then for the final decision, which was vital for the overall appearance of the finished project: with what should we cover the concrete base and plinth to harmonise with and not distract from the bronze sculpture? After much perusing around O'Connell Stoneworks in nearby Killeady, we finally decided on Liscannor stone as the most natural background to blend in with the high stone wall behind the sculpture while at the same time not distracting from the bronze sculpture. Local tiler Pat O'Mahony with two of his workers completed the job in two days. We were ready for the arrival of 'Our Boy'.

13

All She Had
Was Hope

He had a face full of kindness. This, despite the fact that he had few pain-free days. He and his half-twin had a medical disorder that made movement slow and painful. My last memory of him is of his struggle to get up the altar steps to say Mass in St Patrick's, Upton, where he and his twin brother were both Rosminian priests. I knew little about him except that his name was Fr John O'Shea and that he was a native of County Kerry. He was a gentle and inspirational man, who one day during one of our chats gave me a leaflet on which was printed 'An Ordinary Day'. You could not call it a prayer, but maybe words of wisdom which conveyed the message of the value of appreciating an ordinary day, of which he probably had very few. Afterwards

I sometimes recalled it when having a good day at home or maybe out with family or friends. An ordinary day was not to be taken for granted. I was often grateful to Fr John and thought of him as my 'ordinary day' man. Both the twins died at a young age and are buried in the nearby graveyard of St Patrick's.

Then one day out of the blue a few months ago I got a phone call and the man at the other end said, 'I am Father Michael O'Shea, and you knew my brother, John, in Saint Patrick's.' 'I knew him well,' I said in surprise, 'but I never knew that there were three of you.' 'Oh, I am here too,' he laughed, 'and I know that you were friendly with John because he sometimes talked about you.' 'I have great memories of him,' I told this brother, whom I had never known existed, and asked, 'Were you in Upton too?' 'I was, but not for long because I spent time teaching in America and then was out in our mission in Tanzania,' he told me. 'Oh I knew that Upton were very involved out in Tanzania with a huge mission effort building houses, schools and hospitals,' I said. 'Well, it's about that I am ringing you, actually,' he told me as I wondered where this conversation was going, though I was happy to be talking to this brother of Fr John of whom I had such good memories.

'Well, as you know, due to our dwindling numbers it is no longer possible for us Rosminians to be as active out there as we once were. I left Tanzania in 1991 but Tanzania has never left me,' he said. And the way he said those words made me realise that this man's heart was still with the people of Tanzania. 'The local nuns and priests are doing an amazing job despite the crippling poverty of the people,' he continued. 'Nobody can pay for anything so they are dependent on any outside help they can get. Because I was once a teacher, I have a pension and give them as much as possible and help in every way I can. And then last year while out there I got very ill and became a patient in their hospital where they nursed me back to full health. When I was leaving I asked the woman in charge, Sr Flora, who has no English – but I, of course, speak their language – so I asked her what it was that she most needed. She told me an Xray machine. Unbelievable, but up to the previous month she was running this hospital without an Xray machine. She had scraped up enough to pay a deposit of about one hundred euros, but a machine would cost 123,000 euros, which, of course, was far above and beyond her ability to acquire. But she was praying for a miracle to happen. And she asked me to help. So when I came back I set up a GoFundMe and now we have 30,000 euros, but we are still far short of the balance.' 'She must be an amazing woman,' I interjected. 'All of that,' he told me, 'and that is why I am ringing you. The people around Innishannon have always had a great relationship with the Rosminians so I was wondering could you round up some help for Sr Flora so that she could pay off the balance on her Xray machine? Otherwise the people who supplied it are threatening to come and take it away.' 'Of course we will do the best we can,' I assured him, wondering where would I begin with all this. After a few more pleasantries the phone-call ended.

Then I sat for a while thinking of Fr John whom I had known so many years earlier and who would have been about the same age as I was. So, Fr Michael, whom I had never met had to be somewhere in the region of my own vintage, and here was he flying back and forth to Africa, whereas I thought that going in and out to nearby Cork city was a big deal!

But where to start with the money that was needed? In such circumstances a 'Johnny Sound All' is a prerequisite to action: someone whom you perceive as having a balanced view on life and whose opinion you respect. Mine is an old friend with whom I had gone to school and knows me from the skin in, and who had got me over, under and through many a challenge in my life. So I rang her and retold her Fr Michael's story, adding 'We will surely gather up at least five hundred euro.' There was a stony silence from the other end of the phone, and then an explosion: 'Five hundred euro!' she erupted. 'And where in the name of all that's good and holy are you going with your miserable five hundred euro and that poor woman out in Tanzania needing over one hundred thousand for her Xray machine? Will you for God's sake get real. I will give five hundred myself and I expect you to match it, or even double it. And get on to all your old buddies around there. None of you are exactly on the breadline.'

I put down the phone a chastened woman. But also a more realistic one. Of course my Johnny Sound All was right. I needed to think bigger and to work out a plan of campaign. So it was time to round up my usual buddies. I began with members of our Upton Prayer Group, defunct since Covid, but still all friends. My first port of call was Jane, a retired nurse who was flabbergasted at the very idea of anyone trying to run a hospital without an Xray machine. 'That is appalling,' she declared, and I knew that Jane was on the same wavelength as my Johnny Sound All. My next contact actually knew Fr Michael from his time in Upton and had great memories of him. Then another straight-talking woman demanded, 'How much exactly do you want?' and when I named a sum was told, 'Always knew you were a big thinker!' But shortly afterward she appeared at the door with the requested amount and when I thanked her for her fast reaction was told, 'Quickly given is twice given.'

Then I turned my focus to the younger brigade, many of whom are earning good money. Most of them came good. Amongst them was a young man in Dublin who was foot-loose and fancy free and with a very good job. His heart is in the right place, so a phone-call was made and my story told, and then I got the brain-wave of asking him to call to see Fr Michael and decide for himself what he deemed best to be done. I heard no more from him, but some weeks later got a delighted phone call from Fr Michael telling me that he had received a sizeable contribution from this young man. Eventually when all resources were tapped, the Upton/Innishannon collection was sent off.

Soon afterwards my Johnny Sound All rang me and asked: 'What was the name of that priest looking for the money for the Xray machine?' 'Fr Michael O'Shea,' I told her. 'Now, that's a man who knows how to get things done,' she declared, and continued, 'You know on Radio Kerry they call out the death notices? Yesterday I heard a request that in lieu of flowers you could contribute to his GoFundMe project.' 'That's a stroke of genius,' I declared. 'It's more than that,' she asserted, 'because in Kerry they look after their own, so Kerry will come good.'

She was right because a few months afterwards I got a letter from Fr Michael to say that the machine was paid for and all was well. Enclosed with his letter were two letters from Sr Flora, which he had translated from her language to English. One was thanking him, and the other letter was to our group thanking us. Her letter, as well as conveying a huge sense of gratitude, was also full of her unwavering belief that a power greater than herself was working with her. From her letter you sensed that this nun now had the strength of belief that we once had in Ireland. Fr Michael and his team of helpers had planted those beliefs in Tanzania, and they were now benefiting Sr Flora and her poverty-stricken people.

14

The Innishannon
Blackbirds

I deally placed in the centre of the village, overlooked by Dromkeen wood and stretching along the banks of the river, our GAA field fulfils many parish needs. Around its sporting facilities is a riverside walk along which some strategically placed seats provide the ideal location for viewing the wood and listening to the flowing water of the Bandon river while watching the swans sail by. Here too is the Bee Garden, with pollinator planting, and beyond it along a high slope is the Memory Grove where you can plant a tree in memory of people or occasions. But maybe the greatest facility of all is the playground, which daily attracts streams of children and in front of which are seats for parental relaxation and communication. And overlooking all of this is the Parish Hall, which is a hive of communal activity. Sometimes keeping the heart of all this parochial interaction beating harmoniously is a balancing act between endeavour, diplomacy, pig-headeness and sheer grit. The area which incorporates all these multi-layered facilities is known as the Bleach, and thereby hangs a tale which recently took an unexpected turn. Do you believe in serendipity?

Just inside the gate of the Bleach is a long, narrow stretch of land leading down to the adjacent playground. Over the years this has been the home for weeds, clearings, cuttings and horse manure for enriching village flower beds. But last year a decision was reached that something should be done to enhance this very visible area which was not very pleasing to the eye. Due to the historic roots of the Bleach – it was once a field where linen was bleached – it was decided to call the area the Linen Garden. Then it was a case of rounding up the usual suspects, and one fine evening a group of able-bodied volunteers came to do the 'big dig'. Sometimes when one thing moves something else moves with it. Is it a case of the universe responding?

Fortuitously, at this time horticulturalist David, who is part of the team out in nearby Green Piece Nursery, came to live in the village and offered us his expertise with the planting. We filled him in on the reason behind the name Linen Garden and he planned his planting with that in mind. But before planting could commence, we needed a statement in the midst of our Linen Garden connecting the past and the present, and what better way to make such a statement than

in stone. This required a big, natural field stone on which the date of the linen bleaching and the current date could be emblazoned. So, the first step was to find such a stone. We needed a natural, uncut and unpolished stone, one straight out of the depths of Mother Earth. In every parish you have resourceful people and once the word goes out most things can be sourced. And so it was with our stone.

At the southern side of the parish is a farmer, who, at the back-end of one of his fields, has a deep stony glen and a deep ravine where there is an amazing collection of wonderful stones of all shapes and sizes. We were spoilt for choice, though accessibility and transportability had to be taken into consideration. The final choice was a multi-veined, interesting-looking stone with one flat side to take lettering. This had to be hoisted out using a tractor and borne to the village, where, after a lot of shunting forwards and backwards, it was finally deemed to be correctly located. We were then ready for planting.

But David directed that it would help natural weed sup-pression if, after planting, the surrounding earth was covered with sheets of cardboard before being overlaid with thick mulch. So, one afternoon a mini mountain of cardboard was acquired from a nearby fast-food eatery and stacked on standby for post-planting cover. David had his choice of plants ready for collection, which Peter, our dedicated Tidy Towns chairman, collected in his jeep. The planting troops assembled. David had his planting plan layout ready and as he meticulously placed them in position the whole area was transformed. Then the big cardboard cover-up began and this was much more challenging than the planting, but when the cardboard was covered over with thick layers of moist black mulch it disappeared from view. The job was done and what had previously been an eyesore was now a thing of beauty and a joy to encounter on coming in the Bleach gate.

Then as we stood around admiring our endeavours, the conversation came around to Innishannon's linen industry and its historical roots dating back to the seventeenth century, which, now in 2024, had led to the planting and christening of this garden. Oliver Cromwell gifted the village of Innishannon and surroundings lands to one of his generals, Thomas Adderley, and six generations of the Adderley family continued as landlords here until 1830, when it was sold. Maybe the most visual lasting Adderley legacy is their planting of Dromkeen Wood, which was originally planted in contrasting trees to spell out the name Adderley across the hill overlooking the village. This wood, overlooking where we were standing admiring our planting, has been a green and visual blessing to Innishannon. But it was another Thomas Adderley, known as 'The Industrialist', who really changed the face of Innishannon. During his time in the 1700s Innishannon was home to a linen, silk, and cotton industry, all centred around the Bleach. To assist in all these endeavours Adderley invited skilled French Huguenots, then under persecution in France, to come to live in Innishannon, where he built homes for them. Still attached to the

now ruined church at the eastern end of our village, their now roofless Huguenot side-chapel still stands.

To protect his industries and investments, Adderley had his own militia, known as the Innishannon Blackbirds, so-called due to their black and yellow-edged uniforms. In later years Innishannon people were sometimes humorously referred to by neighbouring parishes as the Innishannon Blackbirds Then in 1830 Innishannon and three thousand acres of surrounding land were sold by the Adderleys to the Frewen Estate for the sum of forty thousand pounds. The Adderleys left Innishannon, and the Frewen name, with its connections to Winston Churchill's family, became familiar to Innishannon people. After the Civil War in the early 1920s locals bought out their freehold from this Frewen estate.

When the Civil War dust had settled some members of the Frewen family came back to visit Innishannon. But no Adderley descendant ever came back and the Adderley name, but for the Bleach connection, faded into oblivion. But there is one other relatively unknown link to the Adderleys still with us. This is a silver chalice resting in Christ Church, the church built in 1856, just across the road from the Bleach. This chalice was gifted by the Adderley family. The chalice was actually presented prior to the building of this church when the old St Mary's Church, at the eastern end of the village and incorporating the Huguenot chapel, was still functioning. But although traces of the Adderleys are still with us, no Adderley has ever returned. Then one morning, about a week after the planting of the Linen

Garden, I received a letter bearing a stamp of the newly crowned King Charles. To be honest I smiled to see the head of Charles on the letter because I have always had a sneaking sympathy for him. Not easy growing up when your mother is the Queen and your father sends you to a tough military boarding school to be moulded into something beyond your capabilities. But it was good to see that he had finally got his image stamped on British post!

To my absolute amazement the letter was from an Adderley descendant. To take it in properly I sat down and reread it a few times. The writer had in his possession a large quantity of documents and letters that he felt would be of interest to the people of Innishannon, and he wished to bring them back and donate them to the village. He had enclosed a letter dated 1875 to one of his ancestors from another Innishannon man, John Harding Cole, who had back then recorded much of the local history. I was thrilled that an Adderley had surfaced, and the reason for his doing so was an amazing bonus. Wanting to share my excitement with someone who would be equally excited, I rang my friend Jerry, who had just written a book on the history of Innishannon. In due course, our Adderley man, Paul, and his wife arrived with a sizeable collection of wills, legal documents and papers, most of which were in beautiful old legal script. We escorted him around to walk in the footprints of his ancestors and arranged for him to see the chalice that an Adderley had presented to old St Mary's Church and which is still used in Christ Church. As he held this historic chalice he was visibly moved as the pages of history were turned back. Since then, Jerry and I have pored over these documents that will eventually be entrusted to the care of the Cork City and County Archives. Was it a coincidence that an Adderley returned with the planting of the Linen Garden and while the Charter School, for which his ancestor had given the site, was being commemorated? Serendipity?

JOHN OLLER
Fire
Water
John Connolly
John Grisham
ROBERT HARRIS
PETER JAMES
STEPHEN KING
LOUISE PENNY
GREY WOLF
I'LL NEVER CALL HIM AGAIN
Vogue Williams
UNDER THE RAINBOW
TOM LYONS
Shadow Work
Pat Divilly
The Secret Life of LEINSTER HOUSE
GAVAN REILLY
Amanda Knox
FREE
AUTOCRACY, INC.
ANNE APPLEBAUM
WOUNDS

15

The Blessings of Bookshops

The shelves of our bookshops are oases of tranquility along which we can search, seek and find solace, and sometimes, in the process, exchange thoughts with likeminded book buyers. And often the shop owner may also guide, find and discuss our choices. Or sometimes just the perfect book may be sitting there waiting for you. This happened to me one day recently on going into Bandon Books when a book with a beautiful hare on the cover just jumped off the display table and declared, 'I was waiting for you!' And indeed it was, because this book, called *Raising Hare*, is one of the most beautiful books that I have ever read and every night I became immersed in raising her hare with the author, Chloe Dalton. It's a book to be reread and savoured.

Oh the joy of finding such a book – or maybe of it finding you – in a bookshop. What a loss it would be to the well-being of our society if our bookshops were to be eroded by online shopping.

And even more recently I found yet another memorable book along the shelves of Bandon Books which awakened childhood memories of the extraordinary Monsignor Hugh O'Flaherty, from Kiskeam in North Cork. He was born in the adjoining parish to ours, and his aunt lived beside us on the hilly road down into our town. As children, walking home from Sunday Mass, my sister and I were sometimes joined by this extremely tall man, dressed in black and wearing black horn-rimmed spectacles. He chatted amiably with us as we strove to keep pace with his long strides. My mother and his aunt had long discussions on the best fare to put flesh back on the bones of what to us looked like a half-starved man. It was years afterwards that I discovered that this man was running an underground movement in Gestapo-infested Rome, helping hundreds of Jews escape the death camps. Through the pages of Joseph O'Connor's intriguing book, *My Father's House*, I reconciled the different faces of Monsignor Hugh O'Flaherty. Such is the wonder of books.

At book signings while waiting in queues, customers often chat and exchange book ideas. Over the years of doing book signings myself, I have met the most wonderful bookshop owners and amazing book buyers. Then, some readers wait until the rush is over and come at the end of a book queue to share with you something important to them and they feel you may understand. A writer is so privileged when this happens.

One such experience that stands out in my mind took place in Kenny's of Galway. Prior to that day I had never been to Kenny's but had heard of it through a sister who had purchased paintings in their adjacent art gallery. To have a bookshop and art gallery in the same building is surely a case of having 'jam and jam up on it'. My sister's story about her first visit to Kenny's painted a picture of a very special place. She and her husband had rambled into Kenny's while on a Galway holiday and a Kenneth Webb painting caught her eye. But unfortunately another Webb took her husband's fancy. So, a long, protracted debate followed, and dare I say a marital power struggle took place. Eventually, Mrs Kenny, the renowned proprietor, who had overheard some of this exchange tactfully intervened. She listened quietly to both opinions and then mildly suggested, 'Why not take both paintings home and see how they look on your own wall? That is always the best way to know. And then you can keep the one that you decide on.'

My brother-in-law, a hard-headed businessman, wanted to know exactly how this was going to work. Did they pay for both paintings, there and then, and be refunded on the one they returned? Mrs Kenny serenely assured him that there was no need pay anything yet, but simply take both paintings home and then come back when it suited them and pay for the one they had decided to keep. My brother-in-law was gobsmacked. This woman who had never before seen them was going to let them walk out the door with two valuable paintings with no guarantee that she might ever see them again? How crazy was that? But Mrs Kenny was a wise woman and a good judge of people, and she knew from experience that these two people were honest brokers. She was right and they ended up buying the two paintings.

A few years later I was on my way to Galway to do one of my first book signings for *To School through the Fields* in Kenny's. I was looking forward to seeing this famous bookshop. But you could never be prepared for the wonder that was then Kenny's of Galway. Two intriguing small windows on either side of an ordinary house door gave one the sense of going into a well-loved family home, which indeed is exactly what it was before evolving into a many-roomed shop with book-lined corridors, and shelves all the way up and down the curving stairs. On entry, it oozed a sense of welcoming graciousness, and Mrs Kenny, at the front desk, was the perfect woman of the house. When I entered she looked at me quizzically and asked in a soft Galway accent, 'Alice, have you a sister who lives in North Cork or Kerry?' 'I have,' I told her in amazement because I was aware that in through this shop door every day came people from all over the world drawn by its reputation for literary excellence. 'She bought paintings off me some years ago,' she told me. 'Please give her my regards.' Like my brother-in-law a few years earlier, I was gobsmacked! This really was a woman with her finger on the pulse of this amazing shop.

A book signing in Kenny's was not a rushed affair, rather a gathering of friends and neighbours with much chatting, and no rush. At the end of the queue came a woman who wanted to talk. 'I waited till people were finished,' she said, 'because I wanted to tell you that my mother so loved your book. She was delighted to discover that her way of life had been written about.' In the course of the conversation that followed I enquired as to how her mother was, and with that her eyes filled up with tears and she told me that her mother was in the Galway Regional Hospital with not long to live. This mother was very much loved by her daughter, who was obviously devastated by her impending death.

Later that evening I was back in Kenny's opening a Kenneth Webb art exhibition in the gallery adjacent to the shop. Two paintings in that exhibition remain etched in my memory. One of these was a huge painting of a West of Ireland horse fair. As I stood looking at it, I was transported back to childhood horse fairs in my home town where horses, ponies, donkeys, farmers, jobbers, three-card-trick men, fortune tellers and shawled women jostled for space. The painting was simply superb and brought it all back. The price, if I remember correctly, was about twelve thousand pounds, but in years to come it will be priceless. The second painting was the inside of a forge, and as you viewed it you could smell the horse, smoke and sweat. Two never-to-be-forgotten works of art.

As I stood recovering from the impact of the paintings I again met the woman from the book signing. She too loved the paintings because it had been the world of her childhood and in which her mother had lived. She was very comforted by the scenes. Some pictures can reach out and embrace you.

The following morning, when driving past the Galway Regional Hospital, which now probably has a different name, I decided on impulse to call and visit the woman's mother. Having signed her daughter's books I knew her name and so arrived at her bedside. It was a memorable experience. Gentile and delicate as lace, it was easy to see why she was so loved. We chatted for a while and later I wrote a poem for her called 'The Cobweb of Old Age'. A few weeks later I received a letter from her daughter saying that she had died.

The Cobweb of Old Age

Dear gentle soul
Do not think
You are a burden.
In your love
You conceived them,
And wove them
Into the fabric
Of your life
Giving to them
All your strength.
The tide has turned.
They are the strong,
And you have your
Delicate threads
Caught in the cobweb
That is old age.
They would wrap
You in their strength.
Let them, now,
Because you can
Give so much
Of gentleness
And the wisdom
Of your time.

16

The Music of the Mountains

R ecently I had the unexpected, delightful and mentally stimulating request to write the words for a song
capturing the musical spirit of the barony of Duhallow where
I was born and reared. This would later be set to music. The
request sent me on a journey backwards and inwards.

At the top end of our home farm was a wild area known as
the Black Meadows – black, marshy, rushy land that produced
strong, coarse meadow grass, much loved by the munching
cows, or, if allowed to grow into meadows, became strong,
thistly, crunchy hay out of which long-legged black and
yellow frogs jumped as we saved the hay there. This hay was
full of herbs and nourishment; it sustained the animals well
and kept them healthy over winter.

The Black Meadows were ideally suited for dry hot summers but not ideal in wet weather as they had naturally heavy soil. Beside the Black Meadows was the Glen, which could not be cultivated but was actually the life-spring of the farm because spurting from between its large rocks, bushes, boulders and overhanging ferns came the water supply for the surrounding land. In remote areas like the Black Meadows and the Glen, 'mountain dew' was often brewed, and in earlier times Mass was secretly celebrated by outlawed priests. As the water tumbled down rocky ravines and hit lower land, it changed its tune as it divided itself into less forceful branches, though still strong enough to make their way along the dykes of the lower fields. Here, many years ago, my father pointed out to me the remnants of a *fulacht fiadh*, which had once been the outdoor oven in which venison and other meats were cooked by our ancestors of the Bronze Age. Nearby was a noisy mountain stream called a *glaise*. As it danced down from the Glen, the *glaise*, which had come from the unplumbed belly of the earth, made its own special music as it danced and bounced off stones and ledges. You heard the *glaise* before you saw it.

But when its noisy water hit level terrain, its voice subdued to a lower tone and then turned into gentle streams that murmured quietly as they meandered along. Unlike the *glaise* you needed to sit quietly beside a stream to better appreciate the rippling sound as it crept by. But eventually both the *glaises* and the streams flowed into the river that curved, inch by inch, through the valley at the bottom of

the land. This river, which in the summer hummed quietly along, could in winter raise its voice to a thunderous roar. All these water voices played different tunes.

Beside the Black Meadows and overlooking the Glen was the Fort Field, which encompassed huge ancient mounds where my father, as a young man, had planted trees. This was a haven for wildlife, and from here each morning the dawn chorus filled the valley. But once the birds had heralded in the dawn, the fort became a silent place, and then walking between the ancient mounds you felt linked and yet at a distance from the long-ago world when they had been created. One neighbour regularly walked here to absorb its monastic peace.

But our land was not unique and this entire region, with similar patches of land, was known as Sliabh Luachra, which translates into 'rushy mountain'. St Brigid's crosses were made from these rushes and the scallops of twigs used in thatching were harvested from the sallies along by the river. My grandmother lived in a thatched house and a local thatcher came when the need arose to re-thatch it. It was lovely to watch the faded brown roof being transformed into a glowing golden mantle that seemed to warmly hug the old house.

Sliabh Luacra is renowned as a particularly musical place. Beneath many of these thatched roofs entertainment was home-produced, and these were the culture havens that created and preserved the music along the valleys. House dances were the norm, and here nomadic musicians created and exchanged their tunes. Fiddles, melodeons and concertinas hung off the end of dressers in many of these thatched houses. Gifted fiddle players like Padraig O'Keeffe, The Cliffords and Thade Billy taught and spread their giftedness along the valleys, instructing and inspiring the young. Some sessions were recorded for posterity by far-seeing and gifted radio presenters, people like Séamus Ennis, Ciarán Mac Mahúna, and later Donncha Ó Dúlaing.

Inspired by this history and the sound of the landscape I wrote this ballad of my home place. It will be set to music and performed by Duhallow Choral Group in Newmarket in the beautifully restored church, now the Cultúrlann, in Newmarket town.

Beannachtaí Sliabh Luachra

Sliabh Luachra played its music in the waters flowing free
From the depths of pagan places, holy wells and *fulachta fiadh*
Dancing down the mountains into valleys and green fields
People heard its rhythm and their music flowed with ease.

They played it by their firesides and its lilting set them free
As it tumbled from the hilltops singing songs of liberty
This music of the mountains like a glass of vintage wine
Honed their sense of sacred and appreciation of divine.

It gave them zest for living and of dancing with delight
It helped them see the sun rise in the darkest night
Their music and their dancing and their love of rhyme
Was celebrated round Duhallow in days before our time.

This storied mountain music came down in waterfalls
Seeped into rural crevices and stately concert halls
Vibrating in Sliabh Luachra beneath Cultúrlann lights
Duhallow choral voices scale it up to heavenly heights.

17

Togetherness

An awareness of the importance of mental health has grown in recent years and a current TV programme, 'It Takes a Village to Rear a Child', is showing us the steps required to wean teenagers off their addiction to mobile phones and connect with the world around them. But, unfortunately, this problem in not confined to teenagers. Daily here on our village street people of all ages are so engrossed on mobile phones that they walk past and totally ignore their neighbours. We are not mentally where we are but somewhere else. And we are all guilty. As one wise old teacher once told us 'Sound is heard but example thunders.' And we are thundering! Joyce once referred to a man as living at a distance from himself. Are many of us now doing that? Maybe as we grow older, and hopefully a bit wiser, we wake up to the need for an awareness to be in the here and now.

Many years ago on our farm we had a helper called Dan who came when it suited him and left when he got fed up with us. One day he and a cheeky eight-year-old me got into a war of words during which I disrespectfully called him 'Daneen', by which he was known, though out of his hearing as it has connotations of being little, maybe a bit juvenile, and is a diminutive usually used for child. When I was reprimanded by my mother for such disrespectful behaviour, Dan acidly informed her, 'Missus, children have only what they hear.' That was telling us! But Dan was a shrewd old bird who had learned the lessons of life the hard way.

Maybe one of the valuable lessons that we all learn as we grow older is the importance of our connectedness with others. In the film *Funny Girl*, Barbra Striesand sings: 'People who need people are the luckiest people in the world …' But we will not be connected with the people in our lives unless we take the time to communicate with them and appreciate them. People who have good friends have them because they give friends time – friendship takes time and commitment. Even within a marriage. Many years ago my husband and I were so bogged down in small children, teenagers and business that we had no time to talk to each other. This led one of our friends to demand of me one day in frustration when I had failed to pass on a message: 'Do ye live in the same house at all?' And sometimes I had wondered the same thing.

But one sunny summer Saturday morning, leaving our eldest in charge, we abandoned ship and headed for the hills of Kerry for just one night. One night! It was manna in the desert and we had two golden days just walking, talking and being ourselves. That one night and those two days saved my sanity and taught me a valuable lesson. It is so easy for partners, family and friends to drift apart and there are many, many undetectable, invisible factors that cause this to happen. After that one night and two days away in Kerry I wrote the following:

Togetherness
Kept apart by busy days
We who belong together
As the interlaced fingers
Of praying hands
Join again in quiet times
At peace in our togetherness.

And as we grow older togetherness-time with family, friends and neighbours grows more precious. An understanding friend to lift you up when you are having a bad day is one of life's greatest blessings. One day on the hill beside my house I met a retired lady who had recently moved into our village, and in the course of the conversation she told me that she was finding it extremely difficult to get to know people and settle in. She told me that she had a pain in her face from smiling at people who did not smile back. A sobering revelation. If you move house and you have school-going children you have access to other parents and their activities, but that is not so in retirement. However, in this parish we have a Friendship Club, Yoga Club, Bridge Club, Flower Club and many other clubs and once this lovely lady got engaged with the one that suited her, she was on her way, and now is happily settled into our community.

Maybe in the past a connection point for communities was one of the pluses of our once regular Church attendance. After Mass or church service neighbours met weekly and often stood outside afterwards and caught up with parish happenings, and newcomers were introduced to their neighbours. We miss that frequent connectedness now and maybe we have yet to find new ways to replace it. I was never a pub person but I would imagine that they are a meeting and connection point for many. On our annual Tidy Towns pub quiz night the camaraderie and companionship of the pub is very evident. My husband became an enthusiastic Bridge player when he retired from the frantic world of GAA and other physically committed activities. Bridge became his all-absorbing hobby and within the home club, and indeed with people in others clubs, he formed many friendships. Up to his sudden departure he lived life to the full, and was interested and interesting. One of the greatest tragedies in life must surely be to die in spirit while you are still alive.

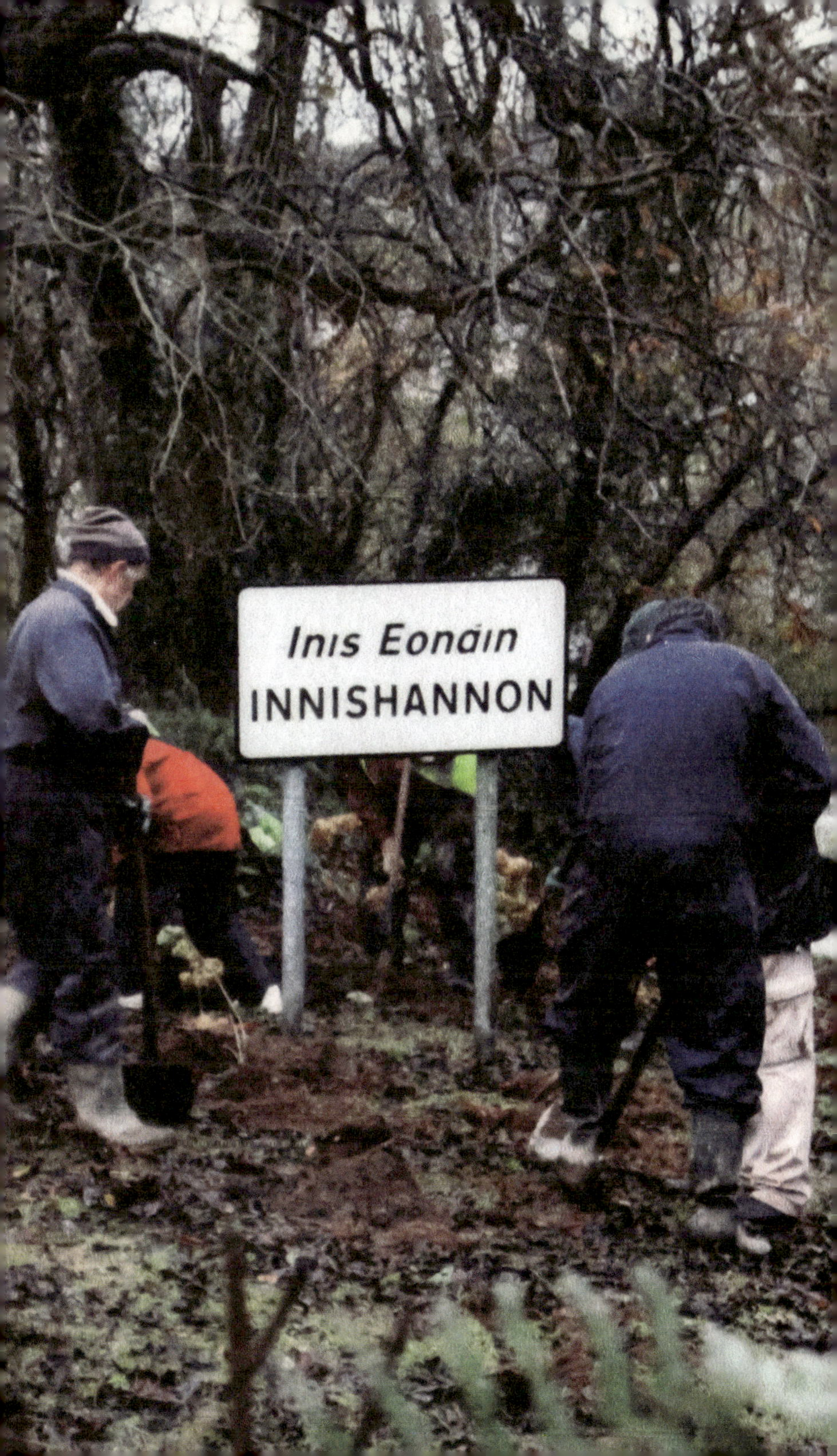
Inis Eonáin
INNISHANNON

18

Build the Nest and the Singing Bird Will Come

On my recent visit to the Bons to acquire a pacemaker I shared a room with a ninety-five-year-old woman who was hugely interested in the racing world, and every day rang a like-minded friend to discuss racing and pick winners for the day. In the course of our many interesting conversations, she informed me that she had backed the winner in Cheltenham and made two thousand euros. But to her it was not about the money but an extension of her huge interest in the horse world. She had once shared ownership of a good horse with a well-known trainer, and that was very exciting. And she was also an avid Bridge player, and a great reader, and happened to have read the book that I had brought into hospital to see me through my stay. So we shared a good analysis of that particular writer. Though ninety-five, and with accompanying health limitations, she was still living life at a pretty good pace. And she did not even have a pacemaker! But her interest in horses was one of the stimulants that got her motivated.

And we all need one of those stimulants and it really does not matter what it is. If I happen to be in the process of painting a picture, my first waking thought is: how will it look in the morning light? Or if writing, to reread yesterday's work – how does it hold up? This can be either uplifting or sobering, but either way it is an enticement for further engagement. Or if there is a project underway, either in the house, garden or village, this can also be a magnetic stimulant to face me forwards. My friend, Maureen, had a lovely quote for when you are deflated and unable to keep going: 'Build the nest and the singing bird will come.' What a lovely concept.

It is similar to the advice one of his creative buddies gave an artist friend of mine who was unable to get back to painting after a death in the family. He felt that for him the joy had gone out of his painting. But his friend encouraged him to simply put a blank canvas on the easel, mix his favourite colours on the palette, pick up his brush and see what happened. He did this with more dogged determination than enthusiasm. However, slowly at first, but gradually, a spark ignited and he began to paint again. The singing bird came!

One of my cures when lethargy descends and I am crippled by inertia is to lie on the couch with a lavender mask over my eyes and listen to a Phil Coulter CD, preferably his 'Serenity'. Or I could opt for James Galway or Johann Strauss, depending on the mood of the day. The music takes me out of myself, soothes my soul, and when I come back to reality I feel more enthused to tackle something that had previously irked me. But there are other days when I need a calming voice and then John O'Donohue comes to the rescue and his wonderful 'Beauty: The Invisible Embrace' collection unties all my mental knots. Maybe one of the pluses of ageing is that now there is the time for such self-sustenance.

My mother, who was not of the era of lying on couches listening to soothing music, had a more practical approach. On dull, dreary days when her spirits were low, she would begin to tidy a cupboard and once she got going and was back into her rhythm, would declare: 'Isn't it good to have the mind on me to do this.' She was probably a bit ahead of her time with this solution as modern decluttering gurus now advise: 'Tidy your house, tidy you mind.' Looking back now, I realise that another one of her coping skills in the midst of her large, noisy household was to go out alone late in the evening into the surrounding groves picking fallen twigs for the fire. She needed that silent, quiet time to herself and later in the evening she introduced that quietness to her chattering family of varying ages by getting us all to go down on our knees and say the rosary. The rosary brought silence and tranquility to her noisy household. Maybe the rosary in our house, as in the houses of many other families at that time, was serving more than a religious ritual.

My father's answer to the quest for peace and quiet, and maintaining his equilibrium, was to walk the fields of his farm every day where he found solace and acquired a wide knowledge and deep appreciation of the balance of nature. He cautioned us back then to take care of nature. Appreciation of nature and meditation were part of our way of life as we walked to school and to Mass and out into the fields to bring home cows, calves and horses. This harmony with nature was being unknowingly nurtured within us. And now, in my slowing-down years, an appreciation of those values is returning.

But sometimes the kindness of another can pick you up when you are down, and I remember with gratitude the kindness of a friend who one day after a trauma in our family came with beautiful knitting wool and needles and got me back knitting. Knitting can be extremely soothing, and sometimes if I feel a bit frazzled I do some knitting or sewing. Then, I know that in today's world very few people darn, but if you like in winter to wear woolly socks then your big toe will eventually decide to make a breakthrough and a darn is the only fence to keep it in. There is something unexplainably therapeutic about darning, sewing and knitting, and such pursuits were once part of daily living. Recently in nearby Bandon, a sewing shop opened up, which must be answering a renewed sense of that need in our society.

We all have days when the world is too much for us and often a walk can do the trick to bring us back on track. Maybe one of the pluses of ageing is its accompanying slowing down, and as a result we become much more aware and observant. One day, feeling a bit deflated, I went out and sat in the garden where suddenly a beautiful butterfly landed on a leaf beside me, and it was as if the butterfly flicked a switch and turned on a light in my mind. Now when out walking, I take the time to stand and listen. Sometimes a bird may be singing on a branch above my head, so I enjoy an outdoor concert. In spring, every day brings a fresh awakening, but each season unfolds its own miracles.

> Spring came today
> And walked with me
> Up the hill,
> Breathing softness in the air,
> Pouring forth symphonies
> Of unrestrained welcome.
> It was mid-January
> And she just came
> To have a peep,
> Trailing behind her
> Along the valley
> Wisps of purple veils.

This morning my friend Mary came with a big bunch of daffodils that now sit on the kitchen table in an old jug

belonging to Aunty Peg. I love that tall, white, elegant jug, embossed with a gold band. It is the ideal daffodil jug. A bunch of flowers on your kitchen table is a joy to behold and each time you walk into the kitchen this visual joy soaks into your inner being. Friends and flowers must be two of life's greatest gifts.

But we also learn about ageing from those whom we watch grow old around us. Mrs C, who was one of the Big House brigade who spent her later years upstairs in a little apartment in our house, taught me a few salutary lessons. One cold winter's morning I arrived in her bedroom with her morning paper and advised staying in bed a little longer as it was such a bad day. But she crisply informed me, 'When you reach my age staying in bed is not an option. You, my dear, must get up because you have to, but I don't have to so I must. Staying in bed is the thin end of the wedge.' So she was up early every morning. And right up to the end of her days she held little cocktail and dinner parties for her ageing friends. Another of her directives was never to complain, and she herself never complained about her pains and aches. I try too, hopefully with some success.

Recently I met an old friend whom I had not seen for many years. Once we had got over the initial delighted exchanges of reunion, my friend, who is a man of the land, stood back and sized me up. He declared: 'Alice, you're weathering well!' I had not heard that expression for years and it brought a smile of remembrance to my face. 'Weathering well' was the language of the land and was often applied to well-made wooden gates and homemade farm fences that survived the test of time and weather, and still looked good. In a restored house near our village the owner had his front door made from the wood of an old oak tree that had grown for centuries in a field beside the house. Whenever I stand in front of that door the term 'weathering well' comes to mind. This door breathes solidity, antiquity and agelessness. It is indeed weathering well, a restful image to keep in mind in our later years as we, like trees, mellow with the years.

A Memory Tree

When I am gone
People may remember me.
But plant a tree.
And I shall lift my face
To the sun for hundreds of years.
People yet unborn
Will find peace
As they walk
On sacred ground
Beneath my sheltering branches.
The leaves of my tree
Will cleanse the air,
And its roots sustain the soil.
Amongst its branches
The birds of the air will build their nests
And bees find nourishing nectar.
Planting a tree
Is a divine inspiration
Providing a kindness
To the earth
And a loving memory
For future generations.

Other books by Alice Taylor

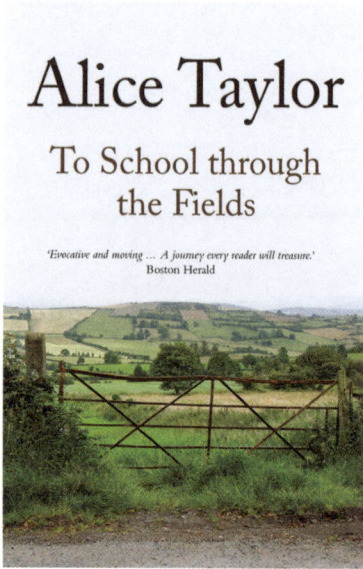

**To School
through the Fields**

Alice's classic account of
growing up in the Irish
countryside, the biggest-
selling book ever published
in Ireland. Beautifully
illustrated throughout and
with a new introduction by
the author.

The Nana

The Irish nana is a repository
of family history, memory
and lore. Alice celebrates
her own nanas, part of the
generation born after the
Great Famine. She herself
is now a nana too, and she
explores the old and the new,
the 'then' and 'now', the nana
of yesteryear and of today.

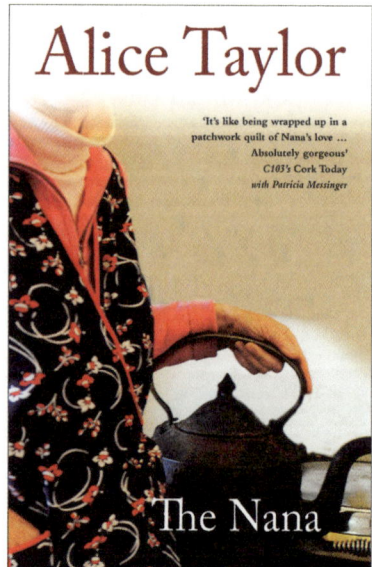

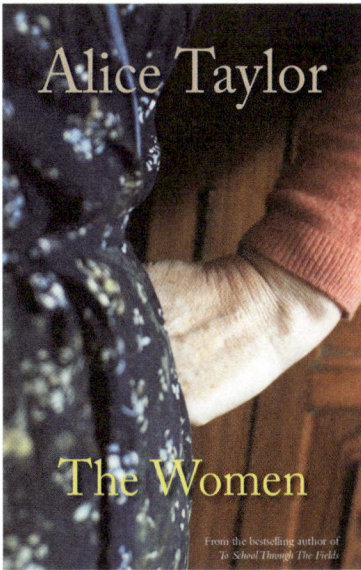

The Women

We walk in the footprints of great women, women who lived through hard times on farms, in villages, towns and cities. This book is a celebration of the often forgotten 'ordinary' women who gave so much to our society.

Do You Remember?

Alice takes us through her home, reflecting on the routine of family life in rural Ireland in the 1950s – a time when food was home-baked and everything was reused. An uplifting account, full of nostalgia and wise words to treasure from Ireland's best-loved author.

Home for Christmas

Join Alice Taylor for the festive season as she welcomes us into her home and shows us the traditions of her family's Christmas. She looks back over her past Christmases as she prepares for this one.

And Time Stood Still

An extended memoir with reminiscences about the author's friends, family members and even beloved animals that have passed away. A therapeutic book demonstrating a compassionate way of dealing with bereavement.

For a full list of Alice's titles, visit obrien.ie